Real America

RICHARD TONG

Copyright © 2024 by Richard Tong.

All rights reserved. No part of this publication may be reproduced, distributed, or transmitted in any form or by any means, including photocopying, recording, or other electronic or mechanical methods, without the prior written permission of the author, except in the case of brief quotations embodied in critical reviews and certain other noncommercial uses permitted by copyright law.

Printed in the United States of America.

Library of Congress Control Number: 2024930167

ISBN	Paperback	979-8-88887-826-2
	eBook	979-8-88887-827-9

Boundless Script Ventures
99 Wall Street #210,
New York, NY, 10005

www.boundlessscript.com

CONTENTS

NATIONAL SPIRIT

American People 1
National emblem 4
New government composition (1784-1819) 8

POLITICAL STRUCTURE

Federal government 15
State Government 20
American political system (1): background 22
American political system (2): political parties 24
American political system (3): general election 27

WORLD ROLE

U.S. economy 29
US interests in the global trading system 36
Strategic goals of the new century in the United States ... 57
This is not a unipolar world—Samuel Huntington 60

AMERICAN LIFE

American character 64
Statutory holiday 69
Etiquette in social situations 71
Gift, date, guest 76

AMERICA AND CHINA

Talking about the development of religion. 80
What US must contain China? Charles Crawheimer. 83
Sino-US Joint Communiqué, 1972 (February 28) 87
Looking at the future of Sino-US relations from the global
strategy of the United States 92
A comprehensive view of Sino-US relations. 104
China and the United States should know each other more. 108

US MILITARY

The United States will update six thousand nuclear warheads. 111
Aegis-class guided missile destroyer. 113
American electric stealth destroyer 115
US 75th Ranger 117
US Navy Seals. 132

CHINESE IN AMERICA

Li Wenhe living in a paradise 133
Illegal Chinese immigrants living in the shadow of the underworld. 136
Management genius Zhang Shengkai 139
AIDS Buster He Day 1 142

NATIONAL SPIRIT

AMERICAN PEOPLE

The American people are a brave and free-loving nation. Originally from all over the world, they were formed by many different cultures, races, and religions. After a long period of coexistence, they gradually became proud of being Americans. Before the 17th century, only the Indians and Eskimos lived in the vast wilderness of North America, but after more than a hundred years of immigration, it has become the new home of the people of European countries, and the most important of them are the 13 state colonies established by the British. The state colonies declared independence from Britain. After several consultations and reforms, the United States of the federal system officially entered the world stage on the eve of the French Revolution. Early Americans welcomed foreign immigrants who made her grow up quickly. The US population was only 3 million in 1776, but now it is more than 200 million. In the process of rapid population growth, the new living space has also been continuously developed, and the direction is from east to west. The pioneers of the extension are not only engaged in farming and animal husbandry, but also in mining and other resources. In the 20th century, the United States has not only become a world power, but also an advanced country in science, technology, medicine, and military power.

Before the colonial period (before 1607)

More than 20,000 years ago, there were a group of wanderers from Asia who traveled through North America to Central and South America. These people were the ancestors of the Indians. When Columbus discovered the New World, there were about 20 million Indians living in the Americas, and about 1 million of them lived in present-day Canada and the north-central United States. Most of the rest live in present-day Mexico and southern United States. About 10,000 years ago, another group of Asians moved to northern North America, which was later the Eskimos. The first Caucasians to the Americas were probably Vikings. They were a group of adventurous fishermen. Some people thought they had been to the east coast of North America 1,000 years ago.

Colonial period (1607 ~ 1753)

In 1607, a colonial group of about 100 people established Jamestown on the beach in Chesapeake, the first permanent colony built by Britain in North America. In the next 150 years, many colonists have emerged, settled in the coastal areas, most of them from the United Kingdom, and some from France, Germany, the Netherlands, Ireland and other countries. In the mid-18th century, 13 British colonies gradually formed, and they had their own governments and parliaments under the highest sovereignty of the United Kingdom. The differences in climate and geographical environment in these 13 colonial areas have resulted in differences in economic patterns, political systems, and concepts.

Independent movement (1754 ~ 1783)

In the mid-18th century, Britain had a rift between the colonies of the Americas and the United Kingdom. The expansion of the colonies gave them some kind of consciousness, consciously persecuted the British, and sprouted the idea of independence. In 1774, representatives from 12 states gathered in Philadelphia to hold the so-called first continental conference, hoping to find a reasonable way to solve the problem peacefully with Britain. However, the British insisted that the colony must unconditionally surrender to the king, and Accept the punishment. In 1775, the war was ignited in Massachusetts, and in May, the second Continental Conference was held, which strengthened the determination of war and independence, and issued a famous Declaration of Independence, which offered sufficient reasons to fight this battle. This is also the last factor to win. In 1781, the US military won a decisive victory. In 1783, the United States and Britain signed the Paris Treaty and ended the War of Independence.

www.richardtong.com.au

NATIONAL EMBLEM

The national emblem of the United States was designed by William Barton and Charles Thomson. The US government began using this country to identify important documents on June 20, 1782. The pattern of the national emblem is a white-headed eagle symbolizing independence and freedom. The front shield-like flag represents the 13 states that joined the United States in 1777. The bald eagle's right claw holds an olive branch that hopes to be peaceful, and the left paw holds a sharp arrow that is determined to defend itself. The bald eagle carries a ribbon with the words "United States" written in Latin. The top of the national emblem is the thirteen gold stars that shine through the clouds.

American flag stars and stripes

On July 4, 1776, the United States of America was born. In order to represent the spirit of unity and independence of this new nation, on July 14, 1777, Congress passed a resolution to formulate the American flag. Since there were only ten states participating in the United States at the time; therefore, the flag consisted of thirteen red and white horizontal bars and thirteen white stars lined with blue. At the same time, the resolution also explained the meaning of the white, red and blue colors of the national flag: white represents honesty and justice; red public represents brave and fearless; blue represents vigilance, tenacity and justice. Since the United States became independent, because the states have joined the Union, on April 4, 1818, Congress passed a bill: "Every time the United States accepts a state, a new star will be added to the national flag on July 4 of the following year." . There are still thirteen red and white stripes on the American flag, and the stars have been added to fifty. They represent the fifty states of the United States.

The American National Bird Bald Eagle represents the brave, powerful and victorious bald eagle (Bald Eagle) TheBaldEagle, the national bird of the United States. The bald eagle is extremely precious, only produced in North America, and now mostly lives in Alaska, USA. The bald eagle first appeared on the flag of the United States during the War of Independence. On July 4, 1776, the Second Continental Conference issued the Declaration of Independence and decided that the new American must have a special national emblem. Later, the parliamentarians spent six years discussing the pattern of the national emblem, and finally selected the bald eagle as the main image of the national emblem. Since then, the Bald Eagle has become the national bird of the United States.

National flower

The rose that symbolizes beauty, fragrance, enthusiasm and love was proposed by Senator John Denn in 1985 and passed by the Senate and was elected as the National Flower of the United States. More than a decade ago, the late Senator Dixon proposed the use of calendula as the national flower. Because Calendula grows only in North America, the 50 states of the United States have this kind of flower. The adaptation of Calendula to the environment and the resistance to pests are also incomparable to other flowers. Although Dixon's proposal was not passed, there are still many "Jinhuai factions" in the House of Representatives. They disapprove of the rose as a national flower, so "rose" or "golden chrysanthemum", what is the national flower of the United States, is still waiting for the House of Representatives to vote.

American National Anthem: Song of Stars and Stripes

In the American War of Defending Independence in 1812, the poet Francis Sgartkai witnessed the British attack on Fort McHenry and the heroic resistance of the US Army in Baltimore. In the early morning of September 13, Francis Kay saw an American flag still fluttering in the wind through the smoke of gunfire. He was deeply moved by this scene and wrote a few lines of poems behind a letter. The next day, he gave the poem to Judge Nicholson, and he was greatly appreciated. He suggested using a song that was very popular at the time as a companion, and at the same time, the song titled "The Song of Stars and Stripes" THESTARSPANGLEDBANNER, This song was deeply loved by the American people and soon spread throughout the country. In 1931, it was officially designated as the national anthem of the United States.

Lyrics

> Ah! At the beginning of the morning, you can see what makes us so proud?
> Cheering in the last rays of dawn,
> Whose banner is always high in the fierce battle!
> The fire is raging, the guns are rumble, and we see the heroic flag on the fortress. It still stands after the night!
> Ah! You said that the Stars and Stripes will be still, dancing on the free land,

Flying in the home of the brave!

www.richardtong.com.au

NEW GOVERNMENT COMPOSITION (1784~1819)

The success of the revolution gave the American people an opportunity to express their political ideas in the form of legislation. In 1787, a federal conference was held in Philadelphia, in which Washington was promoted as chairman. They adopted a principle that the central powers are general, but they must be prudently prescribed and explained. At the same time, they also accept a fact. That is, the national government must have the power to tax, mint, adjust business, declare war, and conclude treaties. In addition, in order to prevent the central power from being too large, Montesquieu's theory of equal rights politics is adopted, that is, three departments of equal cooperation and checks and balances are set up in the government, that is, the three powers of legislation, administration, and justice are reconciled, and the balance is not made. One power takes control.

Expanding westward (1820~1849)

In the early 19th century, thousands of people crossed the Appalachian Mountains and moved westward. Some pioneers moved to the borders of the United States, even to the territories of Mexico and to Alaska and California. The pioneers bravely and diligently seek a better life in the West.

North-South conflict (1850 ~ 1869)

The causes of the civil war are not only economic, political, and military issues, but also ideological conflicts. The civil war exposed the weakness of the United States. A test of the existence of this country. After this test, the United States has stepped into the smooth path of a centralized, modern state. Between the North and the South, there is a dispute over the issue of slavery. The main policy of the South in the national politics is to protect and expand the interests of the "cotton and slave" system; and the northern states, mainly the centers of manufacturing, commerce and finance. These productions do not need to rely on slaves. This economic and political conflict has a long history. In the early 1860s, 11 southern states were separated from the federal government, and another group of governments, the north said that they would not hesitate to pay any price for reunification. In 1861, the civil war broke out. The American face-to-face bloody battle lasted for four years. The south was severely damaged and left a deep scar. In 1865, the North defeated, and this victory not only showed that the United States responded to reunification, but since then, slavery has ceased to be implemented throughout the country.

Industrialization and Reform (1870~1916)

In the early 19th century, the United States began to industrialize, and after the civil war, it entered a mature stage. Less than 50 years from the Civil War to the First World War

In the meantime, she changed from a rural republic to an urbanized country. The machine replaced the manual and the product increased greatly. The national railway network has improved the circulation of goods. In response to the needs of the public, many new inventions are in the market. The banking industry provides loans to promote the expansion of business and industry operations. Therefore, in the nearly 30 years from 1890 to 1917, it was called the so-called "progressive period". In 1914, the world war broke out. In 1917, the United States was finally involved in the whirlpool of the war and tried to play a new role in the world.

The new status of the world (1917 ~ 1929)

In the 10 years after the war, American society and culture can be said to be lifeless, feelingless, and belong to the merchant class for 10 years. According to statistics from 1929, the ratio of living in a city to home is 56%: 44%. At this time, the characteristics of modern life, such as cars, telephones, radios, and washing machines, have become a necessity in life. After the war, the economy showed extreme prosperity for two reasons. One was that the government no longer interfered with private enterprises and had legislative protection, and the other was driven by new technologies. Although the economy has grown rapidly, the foundation is not stable.

The recession era and the Second World War (1930 ~ 1959)

The economic panic has affected not only the United States, but also the countries of the world have been hit by it. The economic panic has left millions of workers unemployed. A large number of farmers have been forced to abandon their arable land, factory shops have closed, and banks have closed down. In 1932, Roosevelt was elected president. He advocated that the government should take action to end the economic panic. Although the new government has solved many difficulties, the US economy will still wake up after the Second World War. After the Second World War, relations between the United States and the Soviet Union have deteriorated. They have stepped up preparations in military, political, economic, and propaganda, respectively. As in wartime, this state is called the "cold war."

REAL AMERICA

Since 1960

Since the 1960s, many aspects of American history have continued to be a continuation of post-war development. On the economic front, in addition to the cyclical downturn, it continues to expand; the population moving from urban to suburban areas continues to increase. In 1970, the suburban population exceeded the population of the city. In the early 1960s, the black issue became the most important issue within the United States. In the mid-1960s, many Americans began to dissatisfaction with the government's foreign policy. In addition, due to the development of the industry, the concentration of the population, and the pollution of the ecological environment in the late 1960s, it was widely noted. In the early 1970s, the economic depression caused by the energy crisis was the most serious since the panic. In the mid-1970s, the economy recovered, but by the 1970s, inflation had occurred. In 1976, the 200th anniversary of the founding of the United States, various celebrations were held nationwide. On April 12, 1981, the United States successfully launched the "Columbia" space shuttle, bringing humanity into another new era of space. In 1985, Reagan was re-elected as president. In the ever-changing history of human development, the United States will start a new page. US jury system One of the important concepts of American law is the jury system, which is also a common law tradition. It is stated in the sixth amendment of the US Constitution that the people have the right to request a jury trial when they are involved in criminal cases; A person who becomes a US citizen is obliged to serve as a juror for free. People who immigrate to the United States must have a certain understanding of this.

The jury has a long history in Western society. As early as in the Greek city-state, the jury system was established and popular. The jury mentioned in Aristotle's famous Greek Constitution is very similar to the current jury system in the United States, which really surprises modern people. At that time, there was no interrogation lawyer in Greece. The people were self-represented. The jurors were also ordinary citizens. They could be said to be real people's courts. At that time, the jury of one case consisted of two hundred to three hundred jurors; the jury of the famous philosopher Socrates consisted of five hundred and one jurors, and the majority of the jurors sentenced him to guilt. Before the trial, each juror was awarded two small metal cards, one casting "guilty" and the other "not guilty." When the prosecution and the defense filed the evidence, the juror made his own judgment, put one of the metal cards into a can, and finally counted the metal card to determine whether the defendant was convicted.

Henry II was founded

Today, the jury in the United States is set to twelve. This was the beginning of England in 1166, when Emperor Henry II was officially established in 1367. The jurors are ordinary citizens who are willing to take a pledge to hear the case in a fair and objective manner. The judges preside over and make relevant legal guidance and then make a collective decision. The jury system in criminal cases and civil cases is roughly the same, but the criteria for judgment are different.

In criminal cases, according to the federal government and most state systems, the twelve jurors in a case must reach a unanimous decision (unanimous decision) before they can decide. (The criminal case in Oregon can be decided by ten-on-two.) The jurors in the civil case can decide the case as long as they reach the majority consensus. Civil jury laws vary from state to state. For example, California is nine-to-three, Oregon is a ten-to-two, and Florida is a ten-to-two.

Another difference between criminal and civil jury is that jurors in civil cases often have to decide on individual issues in the case. English is called "special verdict". For example, in a case, the defendant compensates the plaintiff. On another matter, partial compensation or no compensation may be awarded.

In the criminal and civil cases, what if the jurors are deadlocked and unable to reach a consensus? This situation has occurred in the Greek city-state era. The system at the time was that if the accused was considered guilty and acquitted, the accused would be released. If the jurors cannot reach a consensus today, "Hungjury" is the "unresolved jury." In criminal cases, as long as one of the jurors considers the defendant not guilty, it will result in "Hungjury"; in civil cases, according to the laws of different states, the jurors cannot obtain most of the consensus, and "Hungjury" will also appear; When the judge announced that the case was "Hungjury", the trial was declared invalid. The date was rescheduled and the new juror was re-elected for trial.

Criminal case must be agreed

Why is the criminal case much more demanding, and in a criminal case, the juror must reach a consensus to convict? The legal spirit behind this consensus is that criminals based on criminal cases are convicted, and the punishment involved is criminal. In other words, they will go to jail after conviction and lose their personal freedom. The major cases involve the death penalty, which is a matter of vital importance. It can be said that the fate of the defendant is in the hands of the jury, so the jury must reach a consensus. There is no doubt about the crime of the defendant, and the conviction is fair. This is in principle the same as the trial standard of "no reasonable doubt" in criminal cases.

The principle of the jury system is ideal, but there are also many controversial issues. In Europe after 850 years, with the emergence of Nazi, fascism and communism, most countries have cancelled the jury system. Japan also cancelled this system during the Second World War in 1943. The current jury system is mainly in the United Kingdom and the United States, and 90% of jury trials are in the United States.

Doing a jury duty

American jurors are randomly selected from ordinary citizens, and citizens must fulfill their civic duty to attend jury trials. Employers have the legal responsibility to let employees put down their jobs to serve as jurors. If you do not attend, the defendant will despise the court unless there is a doctor's paper to prove that he is ill or has served as a juror in the past year. Even so, jurors are spending time and disrupting work for many citizens, so not every citizen is enthusiastic as a juror.

The process of selecting jurors in the United States is very complicated and requires a lot of manpower, time and ability. The citizens who were first drawn must go to the court to wait for the selection. During the selection process, both lawyers and judges have the right to ask the candidate's background and opinions on things. (Many Chinese have evaded their responsibilities and have poor English to judges or lawyers. Excuses, try Wanling.), and decide whether to ask him to be a juror. There are two types of lawyers on both sides who exclude the jurors he does not like or think is unfavorable to his own (so the most feared jurors are poor in English); the first is "ChallengeForCause", as long as the reasons are sufficient, the judge agrees that both lawyers Can exclude candidates; second is "no need to exclude" (Peremptorychallenge). The number of candidates that can be excluded is not specified and is determined by the judge depending on the circumstances of the case.

www.richardtong.com.au

POLITICAL STRUCTURE

FEDERAL GOVERNMENT

The national organization of the United States was formulated on the basis of the separation of powers and the federal system and the two major political ideas. When the Constitution was drafted, the excessive concentration of power in individuals or a certain department would endanger the freedom of the people, and thus the legislative, judicial, and administrative The powers are independent and check each other to avoid abuse of power by the government. According to the Constitution: the legislature is the Senate and the House of Representatives and the second-institutional parliament. The judiciary has 11 accused courts, 95 places. Court and 4 special courts. The executive organ is the highest executive head of the president directly elected by the people and supplemented by the vice president. There are several administrative departments. The power of the government is divided between the federal government and the state government. The constitution drafters reserve the state's autonomy to the state government according to the principle that the government must approach the people to deprive the people of freedom. The state governments themselves have legislative, judicial, and administrative powers. The power of the federal government is limited to a state government that cannot exercise alone, such as taxation, finance, defense, foreign affairs, currency banking, immigration management, foreign trade, national welfare, postal services, and development assistance for science and art.

administrative

The government is composed of 12 departments and more than 60 independent agencies established by law. The president is the head of state, the highest executive head of the government, the supreme commander of the various branches of the army, air and sea, and the term of office of the president is four years. In addition to being impeached by the parliament, he will not be removed from the opposition. After the expiration, you can connect to any period. The president and the vice presidential candidates are produced by public bidding. During the term of office of the president due to an accident, when the police can't act, the term of the remnant will be automatically replenished by the vice president.

　　The White House is the presidential palace of the United States EXECUTIVEOFFICEOFTHEPRESIDENT. In order to assist the president in fulfilling his heavy responsibilities, the White House has more than a dozen institutions established in response to the needs of the times, such as the National Security Council, the Economic Advisory Commission, the Trade Negotiation Committee, the Energy Commission, etc. In addition, there are more than ten assistants in the White House. The consultant is always assisting the president. The day-to-day execution and management of federal law is the responsibility of different administrative departments, which are set up by Congress to deal with various national and international affairs. The heads of the ministries are ordered by the president and are often referred to as the president's cabinet. In addition to the 12 major administrative departments, there are many independent institutions. They are called independent institutions because they do not belong to that administrative department. These institutions have their unique founding purposes, and some are regulatory agencies, such as The Public Service Commission, the General Accounting Office, the General Services Department, the Federal Reserve, etc., provide special services to the government or the people, such as the Interstate Commerce Commission, the Veterans Administration, the Securities and Exchange Commission, the National Labor Relations Bureau, and the National Aeronautical Space. General Administration, National Science Foundation, Arms Control and Disarmament Agency, Federal Post Office, US International Exchange Office, etc.

Justice

The judicial power of the United States is endowed with a Supreme Court and a secondary court that Congress can establish and establish at any time.

1. The Supreme Court: the highest court in the United States and the only court established specifically in the Constitution. It is established in Washington DC, the capital of the capital. The number of judges is nine, one chief justice and eight deputies, in thousands of cases each year. The Supreme Court usually only hears about 150 cases. Most of the cases involve the interpretation of the law or the intention of the national legislation. This power of judicial supervision is not a special provision of the Constitution, but a theory derived by the court based on its interpretation of the Constitution. This theory holds that an unconstitutional legislation is not a law, and further states that the interpretation of the law is clearly the authority and responsibility of the Ministry of Justice.

2. Court of Appeal: The purpose of its establishment is to facilitate the handling of cases and to alleviate the burden of the most commercial courts. The country is divided into 11 appeal areas, each with an appeal court, and each appeal court has three to fifteen judges. As the name suggests, the Court of Appeal reviewed the judgment of the District Court.
3. Local courts: There are 89 local courts in 50 states. The litigants can file suits nearby. There are one to seven judges in each local court. Most of the cases handled by these courts are violations. The act of federal law.
4. Special courts: In addition to the general jurisdiction of federal courts, courts established for special purposes, such as the Appeals Tribunal, make judgments on claims for compensation to the United States. The Customs Tribunal has exclusive jurisdiction over civil actions involving taxes or limits on imported goods, as well as courts of appeal and patents to hear appeals against the Customs Court and the US Patent Office. In order to guarantee the independence of the judiciary, the Constitution stipulates that federal judges can serve in good times, in fact until they die, retire or resign. During the period of employment, the judge's offense will be impeached like the president or other federal government officials. The US judge is appointed by the president and approved by the Senate. The judge's salary is also approved by the Congress. The annual salary is from the local judge's $4,600 to the chief. The judge's $65,600 is not equal.

Legislation

According to Article 1 of the US Constitution, the federal government gives all legislative powers to the Senate and the House of Representatives. The Senate is composed of two members from each state. The House of Representatives is divided by the number of people in each state. Each member of the House of Representatives elects a member of the House of Representatives. But there is at least one state in every state. There are currently six states: Alaska, Nevada, Delaware, North Dakota, Vermont and Wyoming, and so on, only one member of the House of Representatives. On the contrary, California has forty-three members.

REAL AMERICA

The early members of parliament were not directly elected by the people. The 17th Amendment to the Constitution, which was adopted until 1913, stipulated that the Senate should be directly tendered by the people. The Constitution stipulates that US senators must be at least 30 years old and become There are at least nine years of US citizenship. The House of Representatives must be at least five years old and become a US citizen for at least seven years. Both of them must be residents of the states they represent. The state legislature divides the state into several congressional districts. A member of the House of Representatives was elected in the year, and a national election was held in each of the two years to elect a senator.

Since the senator's term is six years, he actually only re-elects one-third of the Senate every two years to avoid the dismissal of Congress's function due to re-election.

www.richardtong.com.au

STATE GOVERNMENT

Before the establishment of the federal government, there were individual colonial governments, and later became the state government. Before that, there were county governments and smaller units. Even before the British Puritans landed on board in 1602, they had formulated five. The monthly flower contract, when the pioneers pushed westward, established a government to deal with affairs in each remote area. The drafters of the US Constitution did not change the multi-level government system, although they made the country supreme. But they also wisely recognize the need for a local government, more direct contact with the people, and are more eager to cater to the needs of the people. Therefore, in addition to national affairs such as national defense, diplomacy, and currency, the local affairs such as education and health are classified as local governments. The US state government, like the federal government, has administrative, legislative, and judicial In the three departments, the governor is the chief executive of a state. It is elected by the people. Except for a few states, the majority of the governors are appointed for four years. Except for Nebraska, which has only a single state legislature, all other states have There are two-institutional state legislatures. In most states, state senators are appointed for four years, and members of the House of Representatives are appointed for two years. The state legislature is very similar to that of Congress. The state's judicial organization is not affiliated with national courts. The system, which consists of a group of courts similar to the federal judiciary, handles civil proceedings between private or private and state governments and hears cases involving criminal law.

In addition to the courts of general jurisdiction, many states also have special adjudication courts, such as: probate inspection courts, supervision of wills, juvenile courts dealing with juvenile offenders, family relations courts, handling family discord cases; small complaints court handling Disputes on small debts.

City and other local governments

The United States once dominated the countryside, but today it has become a highly urbanized country. Three-quarters of its residents now live in towns, big cities or suburbs. The need for the city to directly care for the public is greater than that of the federal or state. From police and fire to health education, public transport and housing.

The municipal government is established by the state franchise, and the organization of the municipal government varies greatly across the country. However, almost all municipal governments have a certain type of municipal council elected by the voters to formulate the city's budget, set the fiscal tax rate, and allocate funds. The administrative departments, in addition, they still have the right to veto the city decree. An elected mayor serves as the head of the administrative department. In addition to the mayor and the municipal government of the parliament, there are also municipal government organizations with committees and city administrators. This committee is responsible for the merger of legislative and administrative duties by a group of officials. The number of officials in this group usually has three or more people elected by the public. Each member supervises the work of one or more urban departments, one of whom is appointed as the chairman, often referred to as the mayor. But his power is equal to that of his peers. The municipal administrative bureaucracy was first implemented in Stanton, Virginia in 1908. Under this type, a small elected municipal council made urban decrees and formulated policies. But hire a paid executive to enforce these decrees. In addition to the federal government, the state government, and the municipal government, the United States still has administrative units such as counties, municipalities, towns, school districts, and special districts. The county is usually a sub-district of the state, including two or more towns and counties. In rural areas, county councils or supervisory committees are responsible for collecting, taxing, borrowing, lending, supervising elections, building and maintaining roads and bridges, and implementing national, state, and county welfare programs.

AMERICAN POLITICAL SYSTEM (1): BACKGROUND

After the discovery of the New World in Columbus, the army, explorers and immigrants came to the United States today from Spain, Britain, France and Portugal. In 1776, the British colonies in the east began to rebel. They established an independent state in 1781. The US Constitution, completed in 1787, is the earliest sustainable constitution in the world today. It was completed in the last period of the Age of Enlightenment, which suddenly ended in the French Revolution of 1789. The Age of Enlightenment is an era of conviction for an orderly world. In fact, it is an era of conviction for an orderly universe. This kind of thought has strongly influenced the political system of the United States. It has established three major government systems. The power of each system has a restrictive effect on other systems. No single person or institution has absolute power. Ordered. Congress creates and passes national laws, the president enforces these laws, and the Supreme Court guarantees that these laws are consistent with the US Constitution. Even if the Congress itself is divided into the Senate and the House of Representatives, the number of members of the House of Representatives is determined by the number of members of the state, and the number of members of the Senate is the same for each state. There is also an internal restraint mechanism between them, because one law must have two houses. Pass to take effect.

The president's general term is four years and will not be replaced within four years, even if the party where the president is located in the congress system loses its majority status. The president is both the leader of the country and the political leader of the country. Unlike other countries, there is a king or a nominal president, and the actual political power is in the hands of the prime minister. The dual role of the US president and a fixed four-year term have factors that weaken the political influence of American parties. Under the parliamentary system, political parties choose their prime ministers, but the president of the United States is elected by voters and the state.

If the US president is elected for a second term, he will be in office for eight years. If he died in office, the vice president will be the president. This has happened several times. Since 1788, this way of running for the presidency has never been interrupted, except for the resignation of President Nixon in 1974.

The Senate is two in each state and has a term of six years. The term of the House of Representatives is two years. The judges of the Supreme Court are nominated by the President and confirmed by the Senate. This is another example of a "balanced balance" system and is written in the 1787 Constitution. If the judge of the Supreme Court is confirmed, he or she can serve for life until retirement.

Several senators, members of the House of Representatives and the two highest judges are women. But until now no women have been elected president or vice president.

www.richardtong.com.au

AMERICAN POLITICAL SYSTEM (2): POLITICAL PARTIES

The two main political parties in the United States are the Democratic Party and the Republican Party. Broadly speaking, the Democratic Party generally advocates government practiceism and the workers' movement, while the Republican Party advocates small government, personal responsibility, and commercial society. But these broad differences are often broken in specific situations.

It was not until 1860 when Abraham Lincoln was running for president that the United States did not have a modern political party. At that time, the overriding issue of slavery made the weaker parties leading in the elections have to split because the leaders had to make two major decisions: whether it was unity or the separation of the states of the South from the North. Against slavery or slavery. These issues were decided when Lincoln was president, and the decision was made by the civil war of 1861-65.

Lincoln is the first member of the modern Republican Party. His party is composed of old civil rights parties and members of the Democratic Party who oppose slavery.

The formation of the Democratic Party goes back to Andrew Jackson, who was the first ordinary person to run for the US president in 1828. The reason for unifying this party at that time was its collectivism and led to its modern characteristics of supporting the labor organization and advocating a positive role. The Democratic Party was dismembered by the issue of slavery and the separation of the southern states. It maintained its former characteristics after the civil war, but until now it still has the characteristics of a strong southern movement failure, which has been Its support in the South has laid a strong political foundation, but it has also made it difficult to win a national presidential election.

Before 1860, there was no strict distinction between political parties. The first two presidents, Washington and Adams, are federalists who advocate a simple goal of building a national government that can govern each state. (Interestingly, later Lincoln also held this claim.) The three presidents who started from Jefferson began to be called the Republican Party, but its meaning was to advocate state rights and small national governments. In those years, some people were elected presidents outside of the party. They had no obvious partisan tendencies, such as John Adams, who was elected in 1824, and the then president who was succeeded by President Harrison in 1841. Vice President John Taylor.

During his eight years in office, President Andrew Jackson has established the image of a modern, powerful executive leader, as we believe today the role of the president. His personal reputation has been strengthened by his heroic performance in the 1812 war. Politicians were annoyed by this, comparing him to the king, and for this purpose created a new political party, the Civil Rights Party, which borrowed a term from the British against the royalists. They later succeeded in getting their party into two presidents, Harrison in 1840 and Taylor in 1848, but both presidents died in the early days of their term, and the successor vice president was not a strong civil rights party.

In the following 1850, the Democratic Pierre and Buchanan were elected presidents, but like their predecessors, they were not able to deal with the dispute about slavery and the separation of the South. Finally, these problems can only be solved through war. .

Although both the Democratic Party and the Republican Party have retained their own characteristics, they have continuously changed to a more neutral attitude in subsequent national elections. Because this country is so big, any extreme attitude - extreme left or extreme right - will not win. National majority. Nixon has always been a strategist. He pointed out that the Republican Party must be more conservative in order to win the nomination. After the nomination, it is necessary to change its attitude to neutrality, so that it can be elected as president.

The third party has been constantly appearing and dying until the recent reform party founded by Rose Perot in 1992. Their destiny generally depends on the individual's personality, but no one in the third party has ever been elected president.

The 2000 general elections will likely become candidates for current Vice President Al Gore, Democratic Senator Bradley, Bush Governor and Republican Senator McCain. The results of the selection will appear soon, and may even appear in March, thanks in part to the candidate selection meeting, which will be discussed in the next article.

www.richardtong.com.au

AMERICAN POLITICAL SYSTEM (3): GENERAL ELECTION

We already know who the two candidates for the November presidential election are. Gore and Bush are the opponents of the election, they will compete with each other within 8-9 months before the election.

This was not the case in the past. Past candidates are generally determined by large-scale national conferences, usually in September - just after the summer, before the election. In most cases, the party representatives' meetings in each state will decide who to support, and when they participate in the national conference, they will bring their vote share and bargaining status determined by the population of each state. If they decide not to support a national candidate, they will choose a "the person they like the most", a political leader from their state, so

AMERICAN POLITICAL SYSTEM (3): GENERAL ELECTION

that they will first conduct multiple rounds of voting in the state. Until the end of the generation of a majority of the majority of the leader, then the state's delegation will come to the national polling time to vote for their own votes, so as to choose their own candidates.

For example, in 1880, the Republican Party disagreed on the issue of nominating Ulysses Grant as the third presidential candidate after he took office or nominating James Bryan. In the 34th round of voting, Wisconsin changed its voting method and proposed to increase James Geffid as a candidate. In the 36th round of voting, the state delegations all tended to Ge Feid. In order to welcome the supporters of the Rand and the powerful New York State Senator Roscoe Conklin, the final decision was to choose a New Yorker as Vice President, Zest Arthur. After Gefid was assassinated four months after he took office, Arthur became president in order to cater to the New Yorkers.

www.richardtong.com.au

WORLD ROLE

U.S. ECONOMY

According to current statistics, the American people have reached a high standard of living in the world. The US economic system has been repeatedly blamed, but it does stimulate people to develop resources on the land and encourage them to find newer and better ways. A few companies controlled most of the companies in the colonial empire. Most of them are family companies, which are jointly operated by fathers and sons. To this day, small businesses still play an important role in the US economy. However, in recent years, some companies have grown into large companies.

industry

In the US industry, manufacturing accounts for three-quarters of the country's total production, earning about $450 billion in annual revenue for the country. This number reflects the value of the US manufacturing industry, which does not include raw materials, replenishment fees, and fuel costs. The United States is the world's largest producer, and its factory produces nearly $50 billion more in value each year than the Soviet Union, the world's second-largest producer. In terms of industrial base metal steel, US production accounts for one-fifth of the world's production; automobile production accounts for a quarter of the world's production, meat production also accounts for one-fifth of the world's production, and production accounts for one-third of the world's aluminum. The United States ranks among the world's leaders in cheese, clothing, chemicals, paper, cardboard, textiles and many other manufactured goods. In the printing and publishing industries, the United States is also a leading country. Its largest manufacturing industry is the first in machinery manufacturing, followed by the food manufacturing industry. Other leading manufacturing industries include transportation equipment, chemicals, electrical and electronic equipment, base metals, printing, publishing, paper manufacturing, and metal products manufacturing.

American industrial products are headed by California. This is followed by manufacturing centers in New York, Ohio, Illinois, Pennsylvania, and Michigan. First in the US Industrial manufacturing centers are developed along the New England River. The water from the rushing rivers and waterfalls propels the machines of the factory. Since coal became the main source of power, many factories have moved to coal-producing areas in Pennsylvania or other states. Large industrial cities such as Birmingham, Cleveland and Pittsburgh are thriving due to coal production. After oil and electricity become important energy sources, some industries are no longer located in coal-producing areas. A factory can be set up where there is sufficient manpower or raw materials. Transport functions can also affect the location of industrial zones. Part of the reason why Chicago is the premier industrial center in the United States is that it is located at the top of Lake Michigan and at the intersection of the continental United States. New York City's outstanding transportation function and excellent port make it the largest city and manufacturing center in the United States. The Great Lakes region has also made Buffalo, Detroit and Milwaukee important industrial centers. Two great developments in 1800 caused an industrial revolution. One is the invention of the working machine, and the other is the use of individual parts. Until the 20th century, American industry had never associated these two developments with production lines. When you think of it, a new era of low-cost mass production begins. Henry Ford is the first adventurer to engage in mass production. Mass production has made the United States an industrial giant in the world and has improved the standard of living in the United States. The importance of automation to American industry is constantly increasing. Today, many industries use machines that are automatically controlled. Automated production can reduce the demand for labor, but it makes the status of highly trained technicians and engineers more important. Automated production increases production, but there are also many problems. For example, workers who are replaced by machines must be trained in other occupations, otherwise there will be threats of unemployment. The industry is always interested in developing new products and developing better technologies. In order to achieve these goals, the United States has openly established more than 10,000 laboratories. These laboratories employ nearly 380,000 scientists and engineers, and spend up to $25 billion annually on scientific research. Industrial research is a very important part of the US research program, supported by governments, universities, colleges, and private consortia.

agriculture

The United States is one of the most important agricultural countries in the world. American farms produce $90 billion worth of agricultural products each year. American farmers produce 50% of the world's corn, 20% of oats, and 15% of chicken, pork, cotton, tobacco and wheat. In 1850, almost three-fifths of the working population in the United States lived on agriculture. Today, only 5% (about 4.25 million) are still farming. The vast majority of livestock and food crops and industrial crops in the country are produced by them, and they are also exported. The extensive use of machine and scientific farming methods has made the need for manpower more economical. In 1820, the food cultivated by an American peasant could only supply four people; today, the food cultivated by a farmer can support 56 people. Farmers in the United States use tractors, planters, tillers, harvesters, and other machines to engage in farming. These devices can operate a large farm with very few people. Modern farming methods include improved fertilizers, disease-resistant plants, crop rotation, and scientific feeding methods for livestock. Looking for a surplus in crop production has become an important issue.

About 90% of farmers in the United States own their own land, while others rent land from others. The size of the US farm is quite large, with an average area of 440 acres per farm in the mid-1970s. As farms become more mechanized, the area of farm land continues to increase. During the economic panic of the 1930s, the US federal government issued a series of decrees to protect farmers, prevent low prices, control excess grain, and encourage soil and water conservation. These goals are still an important part of the federal agricultural program until today. The cultivated area of grain on American soil is about 336 million mu. The type of grain and the way it is cultivated vary depending on the climate and soil. In the Rocky Mountains and New England, farmers first planted cereals to support their families. Then, small farms also produce cities with daily supplies and poultry supplies nearby. But in southern California, farmers found that the soil, climate, flat land and coastal plains were suitable for growing tobacco and cotton, and the cultivation of these crops formed a systematic arable land and farm. In the Midwest, pioneers have found that broad, fertile land is suitable for a variety of grains and pastures. Today, this piece of land, which accounts for only one-fifth of the US area, includes 60% of the US grain. Corn is the most important crop in the United States, both in terms of acreage or economic benefits. Other important crops are wheat, soybeans, tobacco, cotton, sugar beets, peanuts, sugar cane, oranges, barley, apples, grapes, and many other crops.

More than a quarter of the US's area is pasture and grassland. The public land of about 11 million acres in the western 11 states is divided into many pasture areas, and private pasture owners can use these pasture areas with the permission of the Ministry of the Interior. Dairy cows and beef cattle are the most important livestock on American farms. Midwestern farms and the Great Western Hills are the most cattle-raising places; the American dairy belts are stretched from New England to Minnesota in the southern United States. Most of the pigs are kept in the corn belts of the Midwest. In the United States, almost every farmer has chickens to supplement the meat and eggs in the home. However, some farmers specialize in raising large groups of broiler chicken or egg chicken.

mining

The annual mineral value of the United States can reach about 60 billion US dollars, of which the value of oil production accounts for almost 40% of the total mineral value. Coal is the second most valuable mineral in terms of oil, and natural gas ranks third. The United States accounts for 18% of the world's natural coal and oil, and 45% of the world's natural gas. The increasing demand for minerals in the US industry is a series of challenges for the mining industry - they must explore new deposits. The explorer once used a crossbow and a shovel to find the vein. Today, however, mining companies and drilling companies hire highly trained engineers and geologists to find new veins. These experts also tried to extract minerals from low-level ores that were once considered useless in a new way. The oil industry is the best example of scientific exploration. Since 1900, experts have been predicting that the United States will soon consume the stock of domestic oil in a few years. However, until today, new oil fields have been continuously discovered. Engineers have also invented a new method of extracting oil, so many abandoned fields have been re-operated.

In any case, the amount of oil used in the United States today has forced her to import large quantities of oil from abroad. Experts believe that researching better technology and making more surveys is necessary to reduce oil imports. The US mining industry has made considerable contributions to improving the work of the pits. At the same time, it also increases the production of ore. Only the Soviet Union and Saudi Arabia have produced more oil than the United States. Texas is the main oil producer in the United States, accounting for 40% of domestic oil production and 6% of world production. Louisiana and California are second only to Texas oil production sites. The United States is also the country with the largest natural gas production in the world. Natural gas produced in Texas accounts for about 40% of total domestic production, and reserves account for 30% of the country. Only the Soviet Union produced more coal than the United States. The largest coal mine veins in the United States are located in Illinois, Montana, West Virginia, and Wyoming. Coal production in the eight provinces of the eastern Mississippi River accounts for approximately 78% of national production. Pennsylvania is the only place in the United States that contains anthracite. More than four-fifths of the iron ore in the United States is produced in Lake Michigan, Minnesota and Wisconsin in the Great Lakes region. These soft ores are transported by rail and rail to steel centers in Chicago and Pittsburgh. One-third of the iron sand used in the United States is imported. The United States produces the largest amount of copper in the world. Produced primarily in Arizona, production accounts for almost half of total US production. Utah is the second largest copper producer in the United States, accounting for about one-seventh of the total US production. Aluminum is made up of 90% of a production called bauxite. In addition, Alabama and Georgia also have iron ore mines. Zinc and lead are often in the same mine. The United States is the world's leading zinc producer. New York State is the largest zinc-producing state in the United States. Missouri is the leading lead-producing state. Arizona, Colorado, Montana, Nevada, South Dakota and Utah contain most of the US gold mines. The major US silver-producing states are Arizona, Idaho, Montana, and Utah.

The United States has the largest volume of trade in the world, and domestic trade is much higher than international trade. Nearly 18 million Americans work in the wholesale or retail industry, and merchants who manipulate these trades range from wholesalers, grocery companies, to local grocery stores. Every region in the United States produces the products that are most needed in the area, and the remaining materials are sold to other areas where they are needed for sale. The annual domestic trade volume of the United States is about 580 billion US dollars. The retail sector is as much as $645 billion. In the mid-1970s, the United States imported $120 billion worth of goods from abroad each year, and exported $115 billion worth of goods. The most important trade object of the United States is undoubtedly Canada. The United States ships one-fifth of its exports to Canada, and Canada returns the United States with one-fifth of its output. Other US trade partners are Japan, West Germany and the United Kingdom. The United States also has trade relations with China, Brazil, France, India, Italy, Mexico, Venezuela and other countries. The UK's premier exports include machinery, communications equipment, food, wildlife, processed products and raw materials (such as cotton, soybeans, ore, etc.). The main inputs are fuel, machinery, communications equipment and processed products.

www.richardtong.com.au

US INTERESTS IN THE GLOBAL TRADING SYSTEM

Testimony of US Trade Representative Basheevsky in the Senate Finance Committee

September 29, 1999

Mr. Chairman, Senator Monihan, members, thank you very much for inviting me to provide testimony on the agenda of the United States in the World Trade Organization.

The agenda for the WTO and US trade in the coming months is a critical period. From November 30th to October 3rd this year, we will host the World Trade Organization Ministerial Conference in Seattle, where I will chair. The conference will be the largest trade event in the United States. At that time, leaders of government leaders, trade ministers, business and labor, and other non-governmental organizations will gather in Seattle. The general public will also pay unprecedented attention to trade and prosperity for the United States. The impact.

At this ministerial meeting, we also hope to launch a new round of international trade negotiations, which President Clinton advocated in his State of the Union address. This initiative may create important new opportunities for US labor, business, farmers and animal husbandry; to ensure that trade policies maintain and strengthen our efforts to protect the environment and improve the lives of workers; and improve the WTO itself so that it More transparent, more intimate, and adapted to the needs of the people.

We are working hard at home and abroad to develop the necessary consensus to define an agenda that is widely supported by the United States and the international community. At the time when the ministerial meeting is still about to be held for two months, the timing of the work of the Finance Committee is very desirable. I look forward to continuing to work closely with your committee and other members of Congress to ensure that the ministerial meeting and the new round of negotiations will achieve the results they deserve and contribute to the United States and the world.

Today, I want to talk to you about our stakes in the world trading system, the ministerial meeting, the results we hope to achieve in Seattle and the new round of negotiations, and the process by which we support the agenda.

US interests in the trading system

The United States is currently the world's largest import and export country, with annual trade in goods and services of more than $2 trillion. As a result, the work of millions of American workers, the income of agricultural households, and the future of many American companies depend on a globally open and stable market. In addition, a strong trading system helps all participating countries to feel the real benefits of international stability and prosperity to complement our security policy of maintaining peace.

This is the basic basis for us to advocate the establishment of a trade system for more than 50 years. Since the establishment of the General Agreement on Tariffs and Trade in 1948, successive Democratic and Republican governments have completed eight rounds of negotiations in cooperation with Congress. Negotiations for each round opened the market for Americans and promoted the basic principles of the rule of law, transparency and fair competition in the world economy. Since the end of the 1994 Uruguay Round negotiations:

Opening more markets and a more open world economy has increased US exports by more than $200 billion. This has made a significant contribution to the rapid growth of the US economy over the past five years and the longest period of peaceful expansion in US history. At the same time, it also brought us high-tech, high-paying jobs, reversed the trend of falling wages in the following years, and actually increased wages by 6%.

The rule of law has progressed and the strong system of dispute resolution established by the Uruguay Round has enabled us to significantly improve the implementation of trade rules. Since the establishment of the WTO, we have filed more lawsuits than any other member, and have won many cases or obtained results that are beneficial to us.

The formation of a guarantee for the stability of the world economy. In the financial crisis of the previous two years, 40% of the world's regions experienced economic recession, and the economies of the six major economies shrank by more than 6%, but we have not seen it yet. The obvious resurgence of trade protectionism, thanks in large part to the WTO members' universal adherence to their respective commitments. This provides the crisis-affected countries with the markets they need to recover and protects our farmers and manufacturing exporters from further losses.

Future work

Despite these achievements, there is still much work to be done in the future. This trading system can be more effective in eliminating trade barriers, with greater institutional transparency, easier access, and the inclusion of new countries. In this ministerial meeting and the new round of negotiations, we will discuss the following topics:

International trade barriers remain high in many respects, including certain sectors in which the United States is leading. Agriculture and services are a fairly critical example. In terms of industrial products, we still face strong tariff and non-tariff trade barriers, which need to be resolved through a new round of negotiations.

Our leading position in the technological revolution, the trade system has created new challenges and opportunities. The development of e-commerce and internet trade is a particularly important example.

Joining the WTO can make an important contribution to the reform of the transitional economy, that is, the Eurasian countries that are emerging from the communist system. Observed from the successful WTO members of Poland, the Czech Republic and Hungary, joining the WTO on the basis of commercial significance will help the transition economies participate in world trade and carry out necessary reforms to establish a market-based The economy thus promotes long-term growth and liberalization.

Future WTO agreements can help the world reduce famine, protect the environment, improve workers' lives, promote health and nutrition, maintain financial stability, fight corruption, and promote transparency and good governance around the world.

Below I will elaborate on our WTO agenda in four areas: ensuring the implementation of existing commitments by Member States; developing successful ministerial meetings and agendas for new rounds of negotiations; and encouraging new members to be absorbed in commercially meaningful terms; Concrete steps that can promote ambitious ideas and have direct effects on the United States and the world economy.

I. Compliance with the agreement

First, we are working hard to ensure that existing agreements are fully complied with. The credibility of the trading system and the value of any new consultations depend on the confidence of WTO members in fulfilling their commitments. We have always fulfilled our commitments in a timely and full manner, and we hope that our trading partners can do the same.

We have already made this clear to our trading partners when we were in Geneva. 1999 was a particularly important year. By the New Year's Day in 2000, WTO members must honor certain commitments under the Uruguay Round of agreements on agriculture, intellectual property, trade-related investment measures, subsidies, and tariff valuation. In the coming years, the final commitments under the Clothing and Textiles Agreement, certain aspects of the trade-related intellectual property rights agreement, and subsidy agreements will be gradually realized. Similarly, the commitment of the Uruguay Round tariffs will soon be fully realized.

These commitments represent a balance of concessions from all parties that have enabled the completion of the Uruguay Round negotiations and the benefits of the negotiations. The credibility of future negotiations will depend on the performance of these commitments. We use a variety of approaches to ensure their performance, including the use of dispute resolution systems and US trade laws where necessary, as well as a commitment to implement technical assistance programs to enable some developing countries to meet the complexities of services, agriculture and intellectual property rights. Requirements.

We recently moved a bill in Geneva to emphasize the importance of implementing existing WTO agreements, such as sanitary and phytosanitary standards, textiles, technical barriers to trade, anti-dumping and intellectual property rights. The WTO's inherent agenda requires a comprehensive and critical review of the agreements, which must continue in the new round of negotiations.

Finally, we are urging WTO members who have agreed but have not yet ratified the basic telecommunications and financial services agreements to ratify them as soon as possible. This not only opens up the market for US suppliers, but also ensures that all members benefit from their commitments and enjoy the benefits of competition, transparency and technological advancement that these agreements can provide.

II. Agenda for the new round of negotiations

At the same time, we are working hard to reach a consensus on the specific agenda of the new round of negotiations.

I. Setting the agenda

Generally speaking, we believe that the focus of the new round of negotiations must be on the issues of greatest concern to the United States; the agenda must be broad enough to benefit all members of the WTO and win support from all of us in order to achieve our goals. Create the best conditions; negotiations must achieve concrete results quickly, without adding more questions to comply with commitments.

In setting specific targets for these purposes, we consult with Congress, agricultural and industrial and commercial groups, labor organizations, academics, environmental groups, state and local governments, and others interested in trade policy. This includes the Trade Policy Staff Committee, hearings in Atlanta, Dallas, Los Angeles, Chicago, and Washington to gather opinions on priorities and goals; and a series of symposiums on the agricultural agenda with the Department of

Agriculture to Indiana, Florida, Minnesota, Tennessee, Texas, California, Washington, Nebraska, Delaware, Vermont, Iowa, and Montana directly listen to farmers, ranchers, and other interested parties interested in agricultural policy And in Washington for continuous consultations with members of Congress, non-governmental organizations, business associations and others. At the same time, we have held talks with our trading partners at many meetings in order to reach international consensus on the negotiating agenda of the ministerial meeting, such as the ministerial meeting of the United States and Africa, the Free Trade Agreement of the Americas, the summit of the United States and the European Union, Tokyo's four-nation conference, the recent APEC leadership meeting in New Zealand, and the WTO discussions in Geneva.

Based on these discussions, we believe that in general, the new round of negotiations should set the following goals:

- The core of this round of negotiations should be market openness, including agriculture, services and industrial products (tariffs and non-tariff barriers), and set some basic criteria to ensure that negotiations can be completed within three years.

Negotiations for this round should also pay special attention to areas where trade policies can promote technological advancement, especially e-commerce.

Negotiations for this round should support and complement efforts to improve global environmental protection and ensure that trade policies create the greatest benefits for the broadest range of workers.

As a supplement and balance to the agenda of this round of negotiations, an advance work plan should be proposed to deal with areas that have not yet reached consensus and cannot be included in the negotiating agenda; and a series of institutional reforms of the WTO should pay special attention to transparency and openness.

The timetable for accomplishing these goals is as follows: In Seattle, ministers will decide on a new round of negotiations, agree on the subject of negotiations, and specify the goals of the three-year negotiations. In order to complete the negotiations within three years, ministers must give instructions on how to negotiate. In fact, the ministerial meeting must allow the negotiations to officially begin in the second millennium, and, as some WTO members suggest, propose preliminary negotiations in the middle of the year, and there are other basic criteria for ensuring progress in the future (as may be a year and a half). After the "mid-term" ministerial review, the negotiations will end at the end of 2002, the agreement will be approved in 2003, and implementation will begin immediately.

In the past few months, we have presented the details of the negotiating agenda at the WTO in Geneva, and submitted formal information on the opening of the agricultural and non-agricultural markets, services, commitments, trade and environment, fisheries subsidies, expertise and trade promotion. proposal. These proposals have led to a clear, specific and easy-to-implement agenda for the new round of negotiations, which reads as follows:

two. Market opening

The core of the negotiations is open to the market, and the scope of the negotiations should include the inherent agenda of agriculture and services, as well as industrial products.

In agriculture, active reform of agricultural trade is at the heart of our agenda. Promoting trade liberalization may create more opportunities for US farmers and livestock families; ensure that food is widely available at market prices, fight global famine, promote nutrition for all humanity; ensure that farmers and ranchers use the most modern and scientifically certified Technology without fear of discrimination; reducing trade-distorting means of increasing pressure on land, water and production can help protect natural resources. To protect this opportunity, we will set the following goals:

Completely abolish and ban all export subsidies set out in the agricultural agreement in the future. This is our priority goal with the Western Hemisphere Trade Minister, all APEC members and the Cairns Group.

Significantly reduce trade-distorting support measures and strengthen regulations to ensure that all production-related support measures are tempered, while adhering to standards-based "green box" policies that support agriculture and trade distortions Very small.

Reduce tariff rates and impose restrictions, including but not limited to zero-to-zero tariff reciprocity initiatives.

Improve the management of tariff rate quotas.

Strengthen the business discipline of state-owned trading enterprises.

By all other members of the WTO, various measures are taken to improve market openness and benefit undeveloped members.

Disciplining to ensure trade in agricultural biotech products is based on a transparent, predictable and timely process.

In terms of services, the US industry is the most competitive in the world, with only $246 billion in service exports last year. The Uruguay Round negotiations created an important set of rules, but in many cases, there has been no progress in the gradual opening of the market in accordance with the industry. Effective market opening and cancellation restrictions can enable US suppliers to increase export efficiency and help solve many of the world's broader problems, such as improving the efficiency of infrastructure sectors such as communications, power and distribution; improving environmental services; An open distribution system promotes trade in commodities, creating new opportunities for manufacturers and agricultural producers; and promoting financial stability through competition and transparency in the financial industry. To achieve these opportunities, US goals include:

Restricted restrictions on a wide range of services, including specialized occupations, audio-visual, financial, telecommunications, construction, distribution, environmental protection, and tourism.

Ensuring the provisions of the General Agreement on Trade in Services, pre-considering the development of new technologies, such as current telecommunications technologies, enabling universities to teach, test and award degrees through the Internet; satellite-delivered home entertainment; and through remote Medical care is delivered directly to advanced health services at home or in rural clinics.

Prevent discrimination against special ways of providing services, such as e-commerce or the establishment of related facilities.

Through a number of general commitments, we study the "horizontal" approach to improving management policies across industries, such as commitment to transparency and good governance practices.

In terms of industrial products, further opening up of the market will enable Americans to find high-paying, high-tech jobs and create economies of scale, enabling US companies to invest more in research and development to improve market competitiveness. The next round of negotiations on broad market openness will be based on the initiative of "accelerating the liberalization of tariffs", which advocates the relaxation of tariffs on eight specific industries and negotiations in accordance with the following principles:

Reduce existing tariff differences.

A tariff schedule that regulates the full compliance of all WTO members.

Develop new sectoral agreements and increase participation in existing sectoral agreements, including zero-to-zero preferential tariffs and coordination agreements.

In recognition of the autonomy tariff reduction measures of member states in the near future, including WTO measures such as information technology agreements and accelerated tariff liberalization, and the implementation of general market opening.

Seeking the Interim Execution Office, with its results as the end of the new round of negotiations, to determine the overall balance of market opening, one of the considerations of the overall balance.

Apply the tax rate as the basis for negotiations and increase the procedures for reducing non-tariff and other measures that affect market liberalization.

All other members of the WTO have improved market openness for untapped member states in various ways.

Third, other crucial issues

Most delegations, including the United States, agreed that the new round of negotiations should end within three years. In view of this situation, and in order to find an appropriate balance between various interests, the views are harmonized, and some issues should be included in the prior work plan (such as corruption) so that member states, including ourselves, can better understand The connotation of the new issue forms a consensus for future work.

In addition, there are several key issues in major market open negotiations, including:

II. E-commerce

The most exciting development in business in recent years has been the adoption of new information and communication technologies, especially the Internet. This has far-reaching implications for reducing commodity costs and improving company efficiency. This technology can also accelerate the development of poorer conditions in the United States and developing countries. The Internet has greatly reduced the difficulty for entrepreneurs, technicians and small businesses in finding customers and managing documents.

The WTO must now take action to ensure that no one will block this new trade pattern. So we advocate a broad e-business agenda at the WTO and other occasions, including ensuring a technology-neutral work plan when developing WTO regulations, and cultivating the ability of developing countries to use the Internet. Encouragingly, most WTO members agree that all e-commerce activities apply the traditional principles of WTO, such as transparency, non-discrimination and prevention of unnecessary trade barriers. What I will also say below is that our top priority is to ensure that electronic space continues to be tax-free, that is, countries do not impose tariffs on electronic transmission.

2. Sustainable Development and Trade and Environment Committee

In these areas, we must pay special attention to trade liberalization that does encourage and support sustainable development. In particular, the trade liberalization approach we promote should be fully consistent with the firm commitment of the government to protect the environment. The principles we advocate here are as follows:

Considering the environmental impact throughout the round of negotiations, President Clinton has promised to consider the possible environmental impact of this round of negotiations, and we ask other countries to do the same. Similarly, we also propose that the WTO Trade and Environment Committee assist in identifying the environmental impact of the negotiations during the negotiation process.

Promote institutional reforms to ensure that the public can monitor the WTO and its work processes, especially in the process of dispute resolution, and provide assistance and assistance in assessing the environmental impact of the new round of negotiations.

Promote trade liberalization in a way that strengthens environmental standards. One of them is that the WTO must continue to recognize member states and have the right to take measures in a manner consistent with the promised scientific management principles to achieve the level of health, safety and environmental protection they deem appropriate, even if these levels exceed international standards.

Identify and take advantage of the "two-in-one" opportunity to open up the market and reduce or eliminate subsidies to bring direct environmental benefits. Opportunities we have identified include the elimination of tariffs on environmentally friendly goods through the "accelerated tariff liberalization" initiative, the liberalization of trade tariffs on environmental services, the elimination of fisheries subsidies that encourage overcrowding, and the continued liberalization of the agricultural sector.

Strengthen cooperation between the WTO and international environmental organizations. In this regard, we are pleased to see that the

WTO and the United Nations Environment Programme are discussing ways to enhance cooperation between the two parties.

We have made a number of recommendations in Geneva to promote these goals and are carefully studying other countries' proposals on trade and environmental protection. In addition, when studying other countries' proposals that are not related to trade and environmental issues, we will also consider their relationship to the environment and our high level of environmental protection. In all of this work, we welcome your committee and relevant people to provide valuable advice.

3. Trade and labor

The relationship between trade and labour is also a priority that should be given priority. As President Clinton gave a speech to the ILO meeting in June: "We must make the global economy human and let the workers around the world feel that its successful development is related to the personal interests of the individual, so that they can all benefit. To provide their families with the basic conditions of a just society."

Trade policy can help achieve this ideal. The development of the trading system must be combined with efforts to ensure compliance with internationally recognized major labour standards. The WTO system must bring the greatest benefits to the working people of all countries as much as possible. Consistent with the statutory conditions of the Uruguay Round Agreement Law, we are working to bring international consensus on the trade and labour relations issues discussed by the WTO.

In the declaration of the first WTO Ministerial Conference in Singapore, Member States reaffirmed their commitment to comply with key labor standards. This is the first time that the trade ministers of various countries have officially mentioned labor standards. This first step is of course very important, but we believe that when governments and enterprises strive to cope with the complex issues of economic adjustment and globalization, they should pay more attention to the interweaving of trade and major labor standards. We also believe that the WTO can play an important role in this regard. We are continuing to discuss with the US Congress and the labor community, as well as WTO members that share our interests, to explore the contribution that the WTO can make to this goal.

We submitted a proposal in January to recommend a work plan in the WTO to deal with trade issues related to labor standards, and to study the use of further information by WTO members, and to analyze this relationship and the development of the ILO. The benefits that can be obtained. In addition, we hope to strengthen the links between the ILO and the WTO through the exchange of observers in order to cooperate on issues of common interest to both organizations. We will discuss these issues with your committee in the coming months.

Of course, the work of the WTO on these issues is a broader effort centered on the ILO. Under the leadership of the President, the epoch-making Convention on the Elimination of the Worst Forms of Child Labour has recently been concluded. This is another achievement after the Declaration of Fundamental Principles and Rights in June 1998, which covers core labor standards and follow-up mechanisms. In support of this work, the President referred to the "Major Labor Standards and Social Safety Network Initiative" in the 1999 State of the Union address, including requesting a budget of $25 million to provide multilateral assistance through the ILO. Some countries provide basic labor protection and improve working conditions. Of course, we also use the labor policy tools of trade regulations, especially the traditional conditions of the general tariff system, to promote compliance with key labor standards.

4. Institutional reform

The experience of the WTO over the past five years shows that its structure needs to be further strengthened in some aspects. It should be more fully embodies the basic principles of transparency, adapting to the needs of the people, and being accessible to the public. It is necessary to further ensure that the operation of the WTO and the work of international organizations in related fields support each other in order to promote construction more effectively and make the world economy more prosperous, sustainable and fair. Therefore, we have proposed a series of reform proposals to enable the WTO to perform its policy functions more effectively, while strengthening the public's support base for the WTO. These recommendations include:

Institutional reforms that enhance transparency and secure public support for the WTO by:

Improve the way people connect with the delegation and the WTO.

Enhance the transparency of the work process, especially the dispute resolution process, and disseminate information about WTO issues and activities to the greatest extent possible.

Develop expertise to ensure that member states with low levels of development in the WTO have the ability to meet their commitments and take advantage of market opportunities. In order to ensure technical assistance and expertise development programs that meet the actual needs and experience of these countries, we have conducted close consultations with our partners in Geneva. This has its benefits because it can help these countries develop and provide a better market for US goods and services. The specific content is:

Improve cooperation and coordination among international organizations in identifying and providing technical assistance to improve efficiency.

Further develop the concept of "integrated architecture" to assist undeveloped countries in implementing commitments.

Ensure that the resources of the technical assistance program are used most efficiently.

Strengthen expertise in management and other infrastructure needs.

Explore the development of a partnership program for untapped countries.

Simplify trade procedures to ensure that US SMEs and low-developing economies can take advantage of the market opening commitments made in this round of negotiations. The objectives in this regard include:

Clarify and strengthen the transparency requirements of the WTO Agreement.

Help improve global tariff procedures to increase transparency and accelerate the distribution of goods so that our exports can enter foreign markets faster and more smoothly.

III. Ministerial meeting

In the coming months, we will reach a consensus with our trading partners on the agenda, including timing issues and the basic criteria set to ensure the start and end of the negotiations on time, to prepare for the success of the Seattle Conference. And consult with your committee and Congress on all these issues. We also hope to reach agreement on several initiatives that will lay the foundation for the success of this round of negotiations and use existing opportunities to open markets and reform the WTO. Includes the following:

First, absorb new members

It is very important to absorb new members to join the WTO on the basis of commercial significance, and to build a fair, open and prosperous world economy.

Seven new members have joined the WTO since 1995: Bulgaria, Ecuador, Kyrgyzstan, Latvia, Mongolia, Panama and Slovenia. Estonia and Georgia have also completed negotiations. They all reach important agreements of commercial significance. There are also 31 countries that have applied, and we expect new countries to join the WTO in accordance with the same principles in the coming months. This year we have completed bilateral negotiations with Taiwan, and there have been significant progress in the membership of Albania, Armenia, Croatia, Jordan, Lithuania, Madawa and Oman. We also hold important and fruitful talks with Russia, Saudi Arabia and Ukraine. We hope to complete negotiations with some countries in November.

Of course, the work of the WTO on these issues is a broader effort centered on the ILO. Under the leadership of the President, the epoch-making Convention on the Elimination of the Worst Forms of Child Labour has recently been concluded. This is another achievement after the Declaration of Fundamental Principles and Rights in June 1998. The declaration involves core labor standards and follow-up mechanisms. In support of this work, the President referred to the "Major Labor Standards and Social Safety Network Initiative" in the 1999 State of the Union address, including requesting a budget of $25 million to provide multilateral assistance through the ILO. Some countries provide basic labor protection and improve working conditions. Of course, we also use the labor policy tools of trade regulations, especially the traditional conditions of the general tariff system, to promote compliance with major labor standards.

4. Institutional reform

The experience of the WTO over the past five years shows that its structure needs to be further strengthened in some aspects. It should be made to fully reflect the basic principles of transparency, adaptation to the needs of the people, and easy access for the people. It is necessary to further ensure that the operation of the WTO and the work of international organizations in related fields support each other in order to promote construction more effectively and make the world economy more prosperous, sustainable and fair.

Therefore, we have proposed a series of reform proposals to enable the WTO to perform its policy functions more effectively, while strengthening the public's support base for the WTO. These recommendations include:

Institutional reforms that enhance transparency and secure public support for the WTO by:

Improve the way people connect with the delegation and the WTO.

Enhance the transparency of the work process, especially the dispute resolution process, and disseminate information about WTO issues and activities to the greatest extent possible.

Develop expertise to ensure that member states with low levels of development in the WTO have the ability to meet their commitments and take advantage of market opportunities. In order to ensure technical assistance and expertise development programs that meet the actual needs and experience of these countries, we have conducted close consultations with our partners in Geneva. This move has its benefits because it can help these countries develop and provide a better market for US goods and services. The specific content is:

Improve cooperation and coordination among international organizations in identifying and providing technical assistance to improve efficiency.

Further develop the concept of "integrated architecture" that assists undeveloped countries in implementing commitments.

Ensure that the resources of the technical assistance program are used most efficiently.

Strengthen expertise in management and other infrastructure needs.

Explore the development of a partnership program for untapped countries.

Simplify trade procedures to ensure that US SMEs and low-developing economies can take advantage of the market opening commitments made in this round of negotiations. The objectives in this regard include:

Clarify and strengthen the transparency requirements of the WTO Agreement.

Help improve global tariff procedures to increase transparency and accelerate the distribution of goods so that our exports can enter foreign markets faster and more smoothly.

III. Ministerial meeting

In the coming months, we will reach a consensus with our trading partners on the agenda, including timing issues, and the basic criteria for ensuring that negotiations begin and end on time, to prepare for the success of the Seattle meeting. And consult with your committee and Congress on all these issues. We also hope to reach agreement on several initiatives that will lay the foundation for the success of this round of negotiations and use existing opportunities to open markets and reform the WTO. Includes the following:

First, absorb new members

It is very important to absorb new members to join the WTO on the basis of commercial significance, and to build a fair, open and prosperous world economy.

Seven new members have joined the WTO since 1995: Bulgaria, Ecuador, Kyrgyzstan, Latvia, Mongolia, Panama and Slovenia. Estonia and Georgia have also completed negotiations. They all reach important agreements of commercial significance. There are also 31 countries that have applied, and we expect new countries to join the WTO in accordance with the same principles in the coming months. This year we have completed bilateral negotiations with Taiwan, and significant progress has been made in the accession cases in Albania, Armenia, Croatia, Jordan, Lithuania, Madawa and Oman. We also hold important and fruitful talks with Russia, Saudi Arabia and Ukraine. We hope to complete negotiations with some countries in November.

Of course, the People's Republic of China is the largest country to apply to join the WTO. Our negotiations with China have made remarkable progress in April, but the negotiations broke the Chinese embassy incident in Belgrade, causing the negotiations to be suspended for more than four months. At the beginning of this month, we resumed informal discussions with China. At the APEC Leaders Meeting in New Zealand, we directly obtained instructions from President Clinton and President Jiang and agreed to start formal talks.

Second, the review of the dispute resolution system

Second, in order to safeguard US interests and ensure the institutional credibility of the WTO, it is important to establish a dispute resolution system that can be subject to public supervision to ensure compliance with WTO agreements and clarify controversial issues.

Our experience in dispute resolution to date has been generally positive: we have used this system more often than any other member country and have achieved many successful results. However, the failure of the EU to implement the group decision twice is very nerve-racking. Although we have twice retaliated against the EU in the manner permitted by the WTO, we still hope that measures can be taken to ensure that the losing party must abide by the judgment or it will be subject to timely sanctions. Similarly, we believe that this system should be better adapted to the needs of the people by approaching the public and other methods.

Therefore, as the WTO examines the dispute resolution system, we hope to ensure transparency and timely implementation of the panel's judgment. In particular, we hope to be able to presuppose the group's report materials, disclose the instructions submitted by the various groups, allow the friends to brief the briefing and allow public observers to attend the hearing. I hope that a lot of work in this area can be completed before the ministerial meeting.

Third, e-commerce

As I mentioned earlier, we have started a long-term work plan in the WTO to ensure that e-commerce development is not impeded. Our first priority in the near term is to prevent tariffs on e-commerce. Now no WTO member believes that electronic transmissions should be taxed on imports. Under our advocacy, the policy of "stopping" e-commerce tariffs in May 1998 was confirmed. We are striving to strengthen this policy through ministerial meetings to prevent a huge new burden on this growing trade channel.

Fourth, the market is open

Fourth, we hope to reach an agreement in the coming months to expand market opening opportunities in areas of interest to US manufacturers and trading partners. These include the accelerated tariff liberalization actions that will begin (eliminating or coordinating tariffs on chemicals, energy equipment, environmentally friendly products, fishery products, jewelry, medical devices and scientific instruments, toys, forestry products, etc.), and the Information Technology Agreement II, New products are added to the areas covered by existing IT agreements.

Fifth. Cooperation with other international organizations

Fifth, we are working hard to strengthen the ability of the WTO to cooperate with other international organizations. By supporting observers, conducting joint research projects in a timely manner, making good use of technical resources, providing mutually reinforcing opinions and assistance to the program, and other specific measures to support Economic stability. These international organizations include the World Bank, the International Monetary Fund, the International Labour Organization, the United Nations Environment Programme, the United Nations Development Programme, the Organization for Economic Cooperation and Development, the United Nations Conference on Trade and Development, and more.

Sixth, transparency

Sixth, concrete measures to increase transparency, which involve internal issues within the WTO, as well as global management issues. There are two important tasks in this regard:

The WTO itself: The WTO should, to the fullest extent, ensure that the public can understand and access its meetings and working procedures, consistent with the nature of its intergovernmental institutions. As I mentioned earlier, the procedure for resolving disputes is the focus of the work of this session. The necessary goals include the rapid publication of group reports and the faster lifting of restrictions on the confidentiality of documents.

Transparency in government procurement: The WTO can also help to increase global transparency and good governance. In this regard, procurement transparency agreements can make bids more standardized and more competitive, thereby reducing opportunities for bribery and corruption and helping to ensure the effective allocation of resources. The APEC Trade Ministers Meeting and Leaders' Meeting are very supportive of this goal.

7. Identifying the interests of relevant parties

Finally, with the development of the trade and trade system, people's interest in the WTO will obviously increase. This is evident from the interest of many US civil society organizations (including companies, labor organizations, agricultural producers, women's organizations, environmental groups, academic groups, etc.) in this ministerial meeting and our round of negotiations. We believe this is a healthy trend and believe that it will be beneficial for delegations and WTO staff to listen to the opinions of all parties on the issue of trade policy. Therefore, we are negotiating how to properly invite representatives of these organizations to attend the meeting and express their opinions when the delegation formulates policies.

I am pleased to report that the WTO will convene a forum at the beginning of the ministerial meeting to allow WTO members to engage in dialogue with representatives of civil society. When all preparations are in place and the ministerial meeting begins, it is of great significance to have WTO staff, senior officials of the member states and relevant parties engage in dialogue.

in conclusion

In conclusion, Mr. President, the United States has an excellent opportunity in the coming months.

The first ten governments and the twenty-fifth Congress left us with the tradition of the two parties working together to establish a fair and open world trade system. Because of their success, the labor productivity of American labor is now higher than ever, American companies are more competitive, and American households are more affluent.

In the next few years, we can continue to seek happiness for the next generation, as long as we work together to ensure that the WTO can properly handle new business issues, persistent trade barriers, and issues of public concern. As the host country of the Seattle Ministerial Conference, we have a responsibility to help develop and complete an agenda that will achieve this goal. We look forward to working with members of the Finance Committee to accomplish this task.

thank you all.

www.richardtong.com.au

STRATEGIC GOALS OF THE NEW CENTURY IN THE UNITED STATES

Since the British geographer McKinde proposed [heart zone theory] to emphasize the importance of the geo-strategy of Eurasia (World Island), almost all Western geostrategists have a consensus that Eurasia has become The center of world power, the world island of the global geopolitical hub. Only Eurasia, known as the world island, has enough population, resources, technology and culture to become a powerful power to compete with the maritime powers. Therefore, the maritime powers must use foreign policy to maintain geopolitical concerns and use the influence of Eurasia to create a stable balance of power in Eurasia.

By the end of the twentieth century, the end of the Cold War, the United States was the only world power in history that was not excavated from the Eurasian continent, and the center of the future world stage was still in Eurasia. What kind of global strategy should the United States take? Maintain leadership and the role of world political arbiters? That is, in the new world order after the end of the Cold War, how does the United States dominate this new game on the world island! Zbigniew Brzezinski, a national security adviser during President Carter's book, analyzes the rapid changes and developments in the current world situation in the book [Big Board | Global Strategic Thinking]. The United States must have a forward-looking perspective. Sexual global foreign policy to maintain the United States' leadership in the world and prevent the emergence of a large or hostile alliance that is capable of challenging the status of the United States. Based on the geostrategic point of view, Brine's policy of continuing to maintain the world's order of arbitrators and leadership in the next century. What is the strategic goal of the United States in the next century?

"Our (US)'s primary goal is to prevent the emergence of new adversaries, which may pose a threat to the United States, like the Soviet Union. We must work to prevent any hostile forces from taking control of any part of the world so that it cannot integrate the region. After the resources, it is enough to become a global power (except the former Soviet Union), and other potential countries or alliances, in the longer term, it is possible to develop its strategic goals, have regional defense capabilities, and even further dominate the world. The focus of the strategic objectives must once again be condensed to prevent the rise of any potential, global competitors."

This leaked confidential document from the Pentagon's [1994-1999 National Defense Plan Guidelines] broke the US's grand strategy after the Cold War | and continued to maintain the US's top-notch pattern.

Brine's basic views and policy propositions argue that the mission of the United States is to harness the conflicts and relationships between Eurasia and not to threaten the strategic interests of the United States by making hostile superpowers appear. The United States must promptly formulate a comprehensive and long-term Eurasia geostrategy. In the short term (about five years), it is mainly to continuously strengthen the geopolitical pluralism of Eurasia. Prevent hostile alliances or specific powers from challenging the dominant forces of the United States. In the medium term (at least 20 years), the United States should establish strategic partnerships with individual key countries and promote a system of security across Europe and Asia.

In the long run (more than 20 years), the United States will share global political responsibility with its main strategic partners as an arbitrator.

Buh's specific approach is that at the western end of Europe and Asia, the United States should join forces with France and Germany to consolidate and expand [Democratic Bridgehead]. In other words, expand NATO to Central and Eastern Europe and build a larger security system. At the eastern end of Europe and Asia, it is necessary for the United States to form a close political partnership with politically democratic and economically successful Japan. On this basis, it will take the initiative to engage in strategic dialogue and establish a strategic consensus with China to participate in the Eurasian affairs of the United States. [Oriental Anchor].

The twentieth century is coming to an end. The United States has already become the world's only superpower. No country's military and economic power can compete with it, and no other country's national interests can spread all over the world. How can the United States make good use of history? The golden opportunity to implement the strategy of balancing ideals with reality, Brine's strategic goal of constructing the future of the United States in the next century with McKinda's geostrategic theory of politics, which is indeed a problem to some extent in the study of international strategies in recent years. Geostrategic factors in traditional international relations that have been ignored. With deep education and keen observation, Brine offers a macro assessment of the global strategy. In the face of the new world situation after the end of the Cold War, this new work by Brinell is a person who studies geostrategism. s work.

www.richardtong.com.au

THIS IS NOT A UNIPOLAR WORLD
—SAMUEL HUNTINGTON

Officials in the United States are often used to treating the world as a unipolar world. They boast of the strength and virtue of the United States, call the United States a good hegemon, and teach the other countries how American principles, practices, and mechanisms can be put together.

At the 1997 summit of the seven countries in Denver, President Clinton praised that the success of the US economy could serve as a model for other countries. Secretary of State Albright once called the United States "an indispensable country" and said "we stand tall and therefore look farther than others."

From the narrow point of view of the fact that the United States is an indispensable part of dealing with global issues, the latter statement is correct. But it implies that other countries can ignore it, because it is wrong for the United States to cooperate with certain major powers when dealing with any problem; the indispensable part of the United States is the source of wisdom.

At the end of the Cold War, with the collapse of the Soviet Union, the United States often imposed its will on other countries. This unipolar moment has become a thing of the past.

The two main power political tools currently used by the United States are economic sanctions and military intervention.

However, sanctions can only work if they are involved in other countries, but this is getting harder and harder. In this way, the United States will either proceed unilaterally, regardless of damage to its own economic interests and relations with its allies, or will not implement it, making this a sign of weakness in the United States.

The United States can bomb its enemies with bombs or cruise missiles, and the cost of doing so is relatively low. However, this method alone has a slight effect.

There are three conditions for a more serious military intervention: it must obtain certain legitimacy from certain international organizations, such as the United Nations, but at the United Nations, it faces a veto by Russia, China, or France; it requires the participation of allied forces. It may or may not participate; it may not cause American casualties, and in fact, "non-hostile" casualties cannot occur.

Even if the United States meets all three conditions, it will not only cause criticism in the country, but also attract foreign political and public criticism. US officials seem to be particularly disregarding the fact that the more the United States attacks a foreign leader, the more popular it is with its own people, who believe that he is strong and unyielding in front of the most powerful country on the planet.

So far, the demonization of foreign leaders can not shorten their days of power, from Castro (he has seen eight American presidents come and go) to Milosevic and Saddam. In fact, the best way for a dictator of a small country to extend his term is to tease the United States and condemn him as the leader of the "rogue regime" and a threat to world peace.

Neither the Clinton administration, the Congress, nor the American public are willing to bear the costs and risks of being a leader in the world.

Some advocates of American leadership have proposed to increase US military spending by half, but this does not help. The American public clearly sees that there is no need to consume more manpower and resources for the leadership of the United States. Regardless of how the elites of foreign policy are ruined or honoured, the United States lacks the domestic political foundation to create a unipolar world.

American leaders continue to intimidate, commit to action, and then do nothing. The result is a foreign policy that stays verbally and backwards and is increasingly seen as a hegemonic bluff.

While acting as a unipolar world, the United States has become increasingly isolated. American leaders continue to claim to speak on behalf of the "international community." But what countries are they in their minds? China? Russia? India? Pakistan? Iran? The Arab world? Association of Southeast Asian Nations? Asia? Latin America? France?

Which of these countries and regions regards the United States as a spokesperson for their society?

The society in which the United States can speak, at most, includes Anglo-Saxon countries (including the United Kingdom, Canada, Australia, and New Zealand) on many issues, including Germany and some small European countries on some issues, in some Middle East. The issue includes Israel, including Japan in the implementation of UN resolutions. These are important countries, but they are far from being able to reach the global international community.

On one issue after another, the United States found itself to be isolated, with only one or a few partners standing with it, against most of the rest of the world. These issues include United Nations funding, landmine treaties, global warming, the International War Crimes Tribunal, the Middle East issue, the use of force against Iraq and Yugoslavia, and the cutting of Cuba, Iran and Libya.

On these issues, one side is the majority of the international community and the other is the United States. Countries that believe their interests are consistent with the United States are steadily decreasing.

Although the United States often accuses certain countries of being "rogue states," in the eyes of many countries, the United States is becoming a rogue superpower.

If a unipolar world is inevitable, many countries will make the United States a hegemonic country. But this is mainly because the United States is far away from them and is therefore unlikely to occupy their territory.

Second-class countries in a certain region also value the power of the United States, arguing that this can restrict the dominance of the first-class countries in the region. However, in the eyes of this hegemonic country, this is a good hegemony.

According to a British diplomat's observation: "Only in the United States can we find that the world is eager to get the leadership of the United States, and in other parts of the world, we see the arrogance and arbitrariness of the United States."

In most countries, political and intellectual leaders strongly resist the prospect of a unipolar world, and it is better to see the emergence of a truly multipolar world.

At a conference at Harvard University in 1997, scholars pointed out that elites in certain countries see the United States as the single biggest threat to their society. These countries account for two-thirds of the world's population, including Chinese, Russians, Indians, Arabs, Muslims and Africans.

They do not regard the United States as a military threat, but as a threat to their moral standards, prosperity, and freedom of conduct. They believe that the United States is aggression, intervention, exploitation, arbitrariness, hegemonism, hypocrisy, adopting double standards, pursuing what they call "financial imperialism" and "knowledge colonialism" and promoting foreign policy dominated by domestic politics.

Such a reaction is expected. American leaders believe that the world's things are their business. Other countries believe that what is happening within their country is their business. For example, Mandela said that his country refused to be arrogantly told by other countries which direction to go and which country to make friends with. He added: "We cannot accept the role of a country as an international policeman." In a bipolar world, many countries welcome the United States as their protector against another superpower. In today's world, the situation is different, and the world's only superpower automatically becomes a threat to other major countries.

Americans should no longer act in the world as a unipolar world. The world is not like this. When dealing with any major global issue, the United States must at least have the cooperation of some major powers. The result of unilateral sanctions and interventions is a diplomatic disaster.

American leaders should also abandon the illusion of good hegemony, arguing that their interests and values are consistent with the interests and values of the rest of the world. This is not the case. At some point, US actions promote public well-being and are consistent with more widely accepted goals. But this is not the case many times. One of the reasons is the unique morality factor in US policy.

Just because the United States is the only superpower, its interests must be different from other countries. This makes the United States unique, but in the eyes of other countries, this is certainly not good.

(The author is JM Olin Strategic Research Institute of Harvard University and Dean of Harvard International and Regional Research Institute)

www.richardtong.com.au

AMERICAN LIFE

AMERICAN CHARACTER

Every nation has its own unique character. People often talk about the restraint of the British, the romance of the French, the suppleness of the Japanese woman, etc. Similarly, the character of the Americans has its obvious characteristics.

Anyone who has had contact with the United States will generally think that Americans are warm, cheerful, and accessible. When you first make an American, he will talk to you and even talk about it, making you feel unconstrained; when you walk down the street, you don't care about strangers. Look at it a bit more, he may smile at you and nod his head, or say "Hello"; if your car is anchored on the road, there will be enthusiasts to help you repair; if you are on the street The road, there will be someone who is eager to give you some advice. Residents of the resort island of Hawaii are particularly famous for their hospitality. As soon as you step on the island of Hawaii, you will have a beautiful Hawaiian girl offering a wreath for him. This garland is made from freshly picked orchids and is fragrant. The state of Hawaii is also known as "Aloha State". The word "Aloha" has multiple meanings such as "Hello," "Welcome," and "Goodbye." On the Hawaiian Islands, the voice of "Aloha" is everywhere. Can be heard. Hawaiians are welcoming thousands of guests with fragrant garlands and friendly "Aloha" voices.

Many tourists are puzzled by the fast pace of Americans doing things. The first impression of a person who first arrived in the United States is that the Americans are all in a hurry. People in the city always seem to be rushing to wherever they go, even if they are blocked, they become impatient. At first, you might think that this is an unfriendly expression to you. The bus driver urges you; the store's salesperson is rushing to treat you; you are walking down the street, and the people behind you will walk in front of you. You buy something or go out to eat, no one is talking to you. Don't think that the rush of Americans is unfriendly to you. Usually, the pace of life outside the big cities is much slower. In fact, other countries have this phenomenon.

Americans living in big cities such as New York, Chicago, or Los Angeles often feel that everyone is doing the same thing; they expect others to "push" and are no different from those in Tokyo, Hong Kong, Beirut, or São Paulo. However, as soon as they discover that you are a stranger, they will probably be friendly and try to help you. Many of them were strangers when they first arrived in the city. They remembered how terrified they were when they stepped into a new city. If you need help or want to ask a question, you can find someone with a good face and say to him: "I am from a foreign country. Can you help me?"

At this point, most people will stop and smile to give you directions or answer your questions. But you must let them know that you need someone to help, otherwise they will probably walk past you, and will not notice that you are a foreigner, nor do you know that you need help. Occasionally you will meet someone who is too busy or can't help you. In this case, you don't have to be discouraged, just look for someone else. Most Americans are happy to help outsiders.

Americans value the impression that others have on themselves. They consistently respect those who are liked and attracted by everyone. Therefore, they always hope to have unfettered contact with others and get to know more friends. When Americans interact with each other, they don't like to obey others, and they don't like others to compliment themselves with politeness. Americans are worried that they are isolated by others who are not easy to get close to. This means loneliness for the civilian population; for politicians, it means the failure of the election. therefore. The characteristics of Americans making friends are that they have a very good relationship with everyone. They want to give a good impression to others, but they often lack the kind of knowledge that can be heart-to-heart. An American has made a very pertinent evaluation of this. He said: "Americans can see each other and quickly win the other side. But after a week, they will forget you. They like new things. Like their old cars, they also abandon their friends. No one is faster than us in meeting people, but no one is more difficult than us to build a true friendship."

The second characteristic of the American character is independence. They don't like to rely on others, and they don't like others to rely on them; Americans develop a habit of independent struggle and no parental dependence. On the street, every morning, I can see eleven-year-old boys sending papers from house to house, no matter whether the wind, the thunder and the snow are never delayed. Some girls go to their neighbors to help look after their children. Their parents believe that it is beneficial for them to be self-reliant and self-reliant. Children who grew up under this kind of education have always pursued independence as their purpose. When they are studying, they get scholarships on their own merits and earn tuition by working part-time. When they are adults, they leave their parents and stand on their own feet. Once they get married, they are more independent and rely on their own skills. American society has a place in the life and death field; young couples have children and they are raised on their own. They do not expect grandmothers or grandmothers to take care of grandchildren; when children grow up, families have a division of labor. Generally speaking, cooking Laundry, cleaning the room is a matter for mothers. It is a matter of daddy to repair tools, mow the lawn, scrub the car, set the table, wash the dishes is a girl's business, and it is a boy's thing to pack the entertainment room and manage small animals. However, this spirit of independence in the United States often becomes a tragedy for the elderly. When an old man loses his ability to live, his children and grandchildren who are sweeping the snow are rarely looking after him. There are many elderly people in the United States who are so depressed in loneliness and loneliness that some have even died.

The third characteristic of the American character is to be practical. They don't like the infinite fantasy like the French, nor do they talk like the British. The early history of the United States created their character who was good at adversity, looking at goals, and striving for adversity. They believe that dying to face means nothing, and illusion means nothing. They admire those who are smarter and stronger. They like everything to do it themselves, and things can be solved by themselves. Most Americans know how to use machines, repair electrical equipment, paint furniture, and paint walls. They believe that doing the rough work in these lives is, of course, absolutely not decent. On the contrary, those nerds, fake gentlemen, and talkative short-term will be teased.

Americans are also very pragmatic in money. It takes a lot of money to pay for work, and it is natural for the Americans to turn to help others. So they are clearly calculated in terms of labor and compensation. When you take someone else's car, you have to share the petrol fee; when you use your relatives and friends, you have to pay the phone bill; when you go to eat together, the friends usually pay for each other; even the children can ask for help when they wash the dishes at home; parents go to the children's home. You still need to pay for your meal.

The fourth characteristic of the American character is the special value of success. It is often said that the character of the Americans is formed in a fiercely competitive environment. Living in such a contested society, only the strong can only be in the first place, only to defeat all opponents, is the winner. In the eyes of the Americans. What matters is not the family background of a person, but his own talent and ability. Even a child who wants to excel in school can win the favor of his parents. They also seem to understand that the love of parents is not a natural right, but a loot that is achieved through their own efforts.

If you compare the United States with the United Kingdom, you will find a very interesting phenomenon. In the UK, if you ask someone about your identity, the answer is a long list of ancestors' names and titles. There, the origin of a person often determines his destiny. In the United States, when someone introduces you to someone in detail, they will only say: "This is the author of a bestseller", or "This is a tennis champion of a certain school", and will never make a big genealogy. This is related to the history of the United States. During the colonial period in North America, there was no fixed status and traditional level. A person can only succeed if he succeeds. US President Lincoln once said with great humor: "I don't know what my grandfather is. I care more about what his grandson will become." This is a true portrayal of American characteristics. There are also a feature of Americans, that is, they are not moving well. They are always pursuing novel things, constantly changing the environment, and seeking excitement in adventure. They are never satisfied with a stable life and a peaceful environment; they like sports and travel. Change careers, and move around, and some even like to take life to risk. In the United States, university professors can be managers of companies, and bankers may change to be farm owners at night. Former US President Truman has been a farmer, grocery store owner, officer and lawyer before he became a political figure. President Reagan has also worked as a lifeguard, announcer and film actor.

You may have noticed that the Americans are moving very well. People living in the Central Plains and Midwestern United States often only eat dinner with their friends and drive to neighboring cities of 120 kilometers or even 160 kilometers. They rushed to another town to watch a play or listen to a concert. Many colleges and universities are far away from their homes and relatives; they choose a distant place, just want to "look at another place in the country." Americans like to travel in their own country and like to travel around the world. They always want to know what it is like in the vicinity of the nearby hills or neighboring cities.

The phenomenon of Americans moving is more common. According to statistics: About 40 million people move every year in the United States, and one out of every five households migrates once every three years. This frequent relocation, to some extent, reflects that they are not accustomed to a bland life, eager to see new places, find new jobs, and gain new and successful personalities. On Saturdays and Sundays, you can see temporary advertisements in the United States where you want to move, and sell large and small items in your home. In order to break the silence of life, some Americans even took a blockbuster approach and took life as a play: New York shrugged into the skyscrapers, some dared to climb from the outside; the rushing Niagara Falls, some dare Lying down in the iron tube, down the river; the vast Atlantic, more people dare to fly over the balloon. The spirit of innovation and adventure in the American character is indeed more prominent than other ethnic groups.

www.richardtong.com.au

STATUTORY HOLIDAY

January 1: New Year

January 15th: Martin Luther King's birthday anniversary, the latest national holiday.

Mid-February: President's Day, formerly known as the "Washington President's Birthday Day" (February 22), but his birthday (February 12) was also commemorated in the state associated with President Abraham Lincoln. For the previous states, the rules of the states were different until they were later defined as a unified national holiday, and the time was set on a Monday between the two birthdays.

The last Monday of May: Memorial Day, usually scheduled for May 30, to commemorate the fallen soldiers in the war, it is also the beginning of summer in the traditional solar terms.

July 4th: American Independence Day, commemorating the independence of the British colonies under the rule of the British colonies in 1776.

Monday in early September: Labor Day is also the end of summer on the traditional solar terms.

One Monday in October: Columbus Day, first on October 12, was thought to be the day Columbus discovered the American continent.

November 11th: Veterans Day, first known as the Armistice Memorial Day, commemorates the truce of the First World War.

STATUTORY HOLIDAY

The last Thursday of November: Thanksgiving Day, where family members are to have dinner together, the main meal is usually a roast turkey, and everyone thanks to the blessing of God; this tradition comes from a group of British Puritans who immigrated to Massachusetts in 1620. It is said that they were having dinner with local Indians. The Indians taught them how to cultivate them so they could grow their own crops.

December 25th: Christmas

Other special days

February 14th: Valentine's Day

March 17th: St. Patrick's Day

One Sunday in May: Mother's Day

One Sunday in June: Father's Day

June 14th: National Flag Day

Tuesday in early November: election day

The days of Good Friday and Easter are different every year. They are determined by the roundness of the moon. They are not statutory holidays, but the stock market generally has to close the market on Good Friday.

www.richardtong.com.au

ETIQUETTE IN SOCIAL SITUATIONS

(1) Meet the etiquette and go to the complex

People in the western countries have traditionally set up a cumbersome courtesy etiquette. From handshakes and greetings to introductions to each other, there are customary habits. In contrast, Americans are more casual in their interactions between people. In the United States, friends usually greet "Hello" with indifference. Even if two people meet for the first time, they don't necessarily shake hands. Just smile, just say hello, and they can call each other directly. The name to show affection.

But in formal occasions, people must pay attention to etiquette. Handshake is the most common meeting. In the United States, when shaking hands, the woman first reaches out between the men and women. The man holding the woman's hand should not be too tight. If the other party does not shake hands, the man can only nod and pay tribute. Between the young and the old, the older ones reach out first; between the upper and lower levels, the superiors reach out first; between the guests and the host, the masters first reach out.

Look at each other while shaking hands and take off your gloves. If you have time to take off your gloves, you must explain the reason and apologize to the other party. It should also be noted that when people are too many, they cannot cross handshaking. When women meet each other, they can not shake hands. In the same order as the handshake, when introducing the two people, we must first introduce the man to the woman, first introduce the young to the older, and first introduce the low position to the high position.

(2) Calling the name of the surname

Most Americans don't like to use the name of Mr., Mrs. or Miss. They think this kind of address is too serious. American men, women and children all like to call their names and treat them as friendly and friendly.

When people first meet, they often introduce their names with their surnames, such as: "My name is Mary Smith." At this time, the other party can call her "Mary" or "Miss Smith". It is often the case that the conversation may be called by the surname at the beginning of the conversation, and it will be renamed after a short while.

Sometimes I just met an American, I don't know how to call it, you can just call Mr. or Ms. At this time, the other party will quickly understand your psychology. Enthusiastically told: "My name is James Wilson, and I am good for James." Or "Don't call me Mrs. Smith, call me Sally."

Indeed, Americans, regardless of position or age, always try to call each other's names to shorten the distance between them. A publication in the United States has specifically investigated the problem in 150 industrial and commercial sectors, and found that 85% of them are called only names.

Americans rarely use formal titles to refer to others. Official titles are generally used only for judges, senior government officials, military officers, doctors, professors, and senior religious people. For example: Judge Harry, Senator Smith, General Clark, Dr. Brown, Professor Green, Bishop White, etc. It is worth noting that Americans never use administrative titles such as directors, managers, principals, etc. to call others.

(3) Talk to people and ask about private matters.

In American society, all human behavior is centered on the individual, and personal interests are sacred and inviolable. This principle permeates all aspects of social life. People talk daily and don't like personal matters. Some of the problems are even ridiculous, such as asking about age, marital status, how much income, religious beliefs, votes cast in the election, etc. are very presumptuous and rude.

When the United States sees what others have bought, never asks how much the price? See others go out or come back. I will not ask the last sentence, "Where do you come from?" or "Where to go?" As for how many people are collected, it is even more difficult to ask questions. Whoever wants to ask questions in these areas will be disgusted. Americans often use the phrase "the nose extends into the private life of others" to express the contempt for questioning.

It is worth mentioning that Americans' views on age are very different from ours. In our country, the elderly are respected, while in the United States it is "the old man is not worth the money." So in the United States, older people never like others to compliment their age. On one occasion, Chinese students held a grand gathering in a city in the Midwestern United States. The principal of a local famous university and his mother also attended the event. In the welcome speech, the international students said: "The visit of the old lady makes all of our classmates feel honored." The word "old" is respected in China, but it hurts the old lady. At that time, her face changed and she was embarrassed. No longer appeared at the gathering of Chinese students.

Americans are also very particular about "personal space." When talking to Americans, don't stand too close, generally staying outside 50 cm is appropriate. In general, you should try to keep a certain distance from others when you go to the restaurant or the library. When you have to sit at a table with others or sit next to others, it is best to say hello and ask, "Can I sit here?" After getting permission, sit down.

(4) Social occasions, women are preferred

What is the status of American women in social and political life? But in social situations, they always get extra benefits. Respect for women is a traditional custom of European and American countries. From a historical perspective, it is influenced by the style of medieval knights in Europe; if it is analyzed from a religious perspective, it is out of respect for the Virgin Mary.

According to Americans' habits, in social situations, men must be humbly and love women everywhere. When walking, the man should walk on the side of the road; when entering the seat, the woman should be asked to sit down first; the elevator should be placed in front of the elevator; when entering the door, the man should open the door and ask the woman to be advanced. However, when getting off the bus or going downstairs, the man should go ahead to take care of the woman; when entering the restaurant or theater, the man can walk in front and find a seat for the woman; when eating, ask the woman to order first; when greeting the woman, The man should stand up, and the woman does not have to stand up, just sit and nod to pay tribute; when men and women shake hands, the man must take off the gloves, and the woman does not have to take off. When a woman's thing falls on the ground, the man should help her pick it up whether she knows her or not.

In short, when American men are in contact with women in social contract, they respect each other on the one hand, and on the other hand, they must appear in a protective posture to show the status of men.

(5) Polite language is more and more good

Many people who have been to the United States have the impression that the Americans speak very sweetly, and they never let go of good words, and often make the listeners feel comfortable. Indeed, in the United States, "please", "thank you", "sorry" and other languages can be heard everywhere.

In the United States, no matter who gets help from others, they say "thank you," even if they are treated by the president. In the mall, the salesperson's face always has a smile. When the customer enters the door, they will take the initiative to meet and ask, "Can I help you?" When the customer pays, they will smile and thank. Finally, I will send you away with a thank you. Similarly, customers will repeatedly thank them when they receive the goods.

Americans are also polite in the family. Not only between husband and wife, but also with the words "please" and "thank you" to the children, so the child naturally develops a good habit of politeness.

Americans are also used to saying "sorry" to others. When people have small frictions, a "sorry", often makes the mustard smoke disappear. It is just that there are some trivial things, such as asking someone for directions and walking in front of other people's seats in the theater. The Americans will also apologize. When Americans sneeze and cough in public places or talk to others, they are considered indecent. In this case, they will say "I'm sorry" and ask the other party to forgive.

www.richardtong.com.au

GIFT, DATE, GUEST

Gifts, appointments, and guests are commonplace in people and relationships. The United States also has its own unique customs.

(1) Gift giving

Generally speaking, Americans do not give gifts. Some often appear to be embarrassed when receiving gifts. This is especially true if they happen to have nothing to return. But when it comes to holidays, birthdays, weddings or visits to patients, gifts are inevitable.

Americans are the most popular gift for Christmas. At Christmas, the innocent children were delighted to receive a variety of novelty toys, thinking that this was a gift from Santa Claus. Adults often send books, stationery, chocolate candy or bonsai. Gifts are often wrapped in floral paper and tied to ribbons. According to American tradition, there was a "white Christmas" a few days before Christmas. At that time, people wrapped gifts in white paper for the poor nearby.

Most of the visits are free of flowers, and sometimes bonsai. The fragrant flowers bring a springy breath and give the patient spiritual comfort. In the habit, if you personally go to condolences, usually send the bottle of flowers, do not need to attach a business card; if you ask the florist to send directly, you must attach a business card.

When you send a friend to travel, you often give gifts. Gifts are usually flowers, snacks, fruits or magazines. The business card is also attached to the gift, wishing him a safe journey.

In addition, Americans believe that the odd number is auspicious. Sometimes I only send three pears and I don't feel the Philippine book. It is different from the Chinese. When Americans receive gifts, they must open them immediately, enjoy or taste gifts in the gift-giving face, and immediately thank the givers.

The gift packaging is exquisite, the appearance is magnificent, but it is not necessarily too expensive. Sometimes you open the beautiful three-layer and three-layer packaging, only a few chocolate candy.

(2) Dating

Americans are efficient in their work, and they pay attention to planning their own time every day. What time to do, generally pre-arranged. Therefore, they absolutely do not want someone to come to visit suddenly and disrupt their plans. Only dear friends can be exceptional. Not only in peacetime, but also on Sunday. American society is a battlefield for competition. When Americans are working hard, holidays and holidays are like enjoying the family fun with their wives and children. If outsiders don't say hello, rushing forward, they must be unpopular. Therefore, to visit an American family, ex ante appointments are indispensable, otherwise they will be regarded as uninvited guests and even eat closed doors.

It's boring to go to someone else's home and sit and chat in the open air. If you are not a close friend, you will often be "nothing to go to the Three Treasures Hall"; if you want to go, you should write a letter or call to make an appointment one or two days in advance. If the other party has something, you will take the initiative to make another appointment with you. Some courteous and thoughtful readers also put the envelopes with their names and addresses in the letters sent to them when they write to inform them, so that they can send a reply without having to bother. If you go to an unfamiliar person to be a guest, when you receive the reply from the other party, you will often have to return a letter indicating that you will go to the appointment on time. It is a very rude behavior to miss a contract after a date. Once you have something to do, you should notify the other party as soon as possible and express your apologies. When you go to the appointment, it is best to arrive on time. If you are late, it will be rude to let people wait for you; it is not good to go too early. Because there are very few families with servants in the United States, the room is cleaned up and the meals are prepared by the housewives. Whenever there is a guest, the housewife will arrange the living room and prepare refreshments. If you go early, the housewife is not ready yet, but if you want to come out to receive you, it will cause a lot of inconvenience. On those large formal occasions, punctuality is more important. If you go early, you should wait a few minutes outside and then go in.

(3) Being a guest

Dating should be thoughtful, go to the appointment to be punctual, and be more polite and natural when you are a guest. First, knock on the door or ring the doorbell and get the owner's permission before entering the door. Some people have brown felts for shoe shine at the door. The dirt on the shoes should be wiped clean to avoid staining the owner's carpet. The person wearing the hat has to take off his hat after entering the door. It is very rude to wear a hat in the room. If you are visiting on a rainy day, you should pay attention to putting umbrellas and raincoats outdoors. After the coat and coat are taken off, the owner will take the initiative to pick it up for you. You can be polite. After entering the house, you must first say hello to the hostess, and then say hello to the host. If the host family is full of friends, then just shake hands with the owner and acquaintances and nod to others.

Being a guest at an American home doesn't have to be too cautious. If the host asks you to take a seat, you will feel polite and not sit down immediately. Instead, the owner will feel uneasy and think that the chair is unclean or has other inconveniences. You are not allowed to watch the paper on the master's desk or flip through the documents when you are a guest. Don't care about the antiques in the room, and don't ask about the price of the indoor appliances.

When you are a guest, don't smoke easily. If you want to smoke, you should first ask the ladies present to mind if they want to smoke cigarettes to others. If the owner volunteers to smoke, then even if you have smoke, you must accept the owner's cigarette, and you can not refuse to accept the other. Otherwise, the host will think that you are not happy with looking down on him.

When eating at an American home, if you are not familiar with the etiquette of eating Western food, then the best way is to pay attention to the action of the hostess, and it is not wrong to do what she likes. At the table, people often find an interesting phenomenon: in order to express the same friendly feelings, people in different countries have diametrically opposed arguments and practices. When Chinese people treat their meals, they often humbly say that the food is not doing well. Please bear with me. The Americans have to say, "This is my best dish, I hope you like it." Therefore, in the American family, I heard that the master boasted that the food was well done, not surprising, and praised the hostess's craftsmanship. When the owner of China dials the guests for the guests, the guests always try their best to give them a polite expression. In the United States, this is unyielding. For the first time, the owner will arrange food for you. You don't have to be polite, otherwise the hostess will think that you are not doing well with her dishes. At the table, the hostess is the invisible leader. After serving, guests generally wait until the hostess eats it before they start eating. After dinner. It is also up to the hostess to leave the guest to leave.

It's not too long to be a guest in an American home, so as not to delay the owner's excessive time. But don't leave immediately after dinner, you should talk to your host for a while, then thank you for leaving. If a couple goes to someone else's home to be a guest, the wife should stand up and say goodbye. At a more formal banquet, if there are more guests, they should wait until the older guests or important female guests first leave their words before they leave. If you need something to go first, you should ask the owner for forgiveness and then leave.

If you are not very familiar with the owner, you should give a thank you to the host after you are a guest, or write a short thank you card to the owner, which is more polite.

www.richardtong.com.au

AMERICA AND CHINA

TALKING ABOUT THE DEVELOPMENT OF RELIGION

The vast majority of Americans believe in Christianity, but other religions coexist at the same time. This is for historical reasons. A long time ago, many of those who came to the American continent not far from home and abroad were trying to get rid of the religious persecution in the country. They are full of hope and freedom in the new land. This initial desire gradually formed a preference for religion. Everyone who has been suppressed has tried to show that he is a free man and a sovereign. So they advocated choosing religious beliefs at will, choosing churches and ways of worship, rather than just being authoritative as in the past. Therefore, the founders of the United States have legally defined religious freedom from the very beginning. The First Amendment to the US Constitution explicitly prohibits the establishment of state religion. Congress must not stipulate laws prohibiting freedom of religious belief, prohibit federal and state intervention in church organization and activities, and Americans in each state have the same freedom of religious belief.

However, the constitutions of the states of the United States still recognize the superior status of a certain church for a long time. For example, before 1822, the Massachusetts Constitution provided that only the Puritans had the right to vote. The New Jersey Constitution stipulated that only Protestants could hold public office. Before 1790, Pennsylvania also stipulated that public officials must be faithful to the New Testament and the Old Testament. The people of the Bible.

During the colonial period, the church played a great role in American life. In particular, it has a greater impact on the daily lives of Americans. An entry that does not belong to any church group. It will be in a position of being cast aside, no one will communicate with him, and even his family will be discriminated against. The pastor became the chief advisor to American family life and various matters. A large number of books published by various churches have been widely circulated, and they have been regarded as rumors.

During the alternation of the 19th and 20th centuries, with the break of the rural isolation, the religious system was hit in many ways, and the church gradually lost control of the popular customs. For example, people began to think that marriage and divorce were major personal problems and could not be restricted by the church. In the past, on all secular and religious issues, the pastor was always authoritative, and now this prestige has been lost. With the development of higher education, the level of knowledge of the believers is no less than that of the pastor. Social work is no longer dominated by pastors. The issues of science, morality, and religion are almost universally known, and they are no longer exclusive to the pastor.

At the beginning of the 20th century, 50% of the people in the United States were members of the church, which is roughly the same as today. But more and more people have changed their attitude toward religion. Among the new generation of Americans, it is rare for people to hold family prayers and familiarity with the Bible. Religious precepts are no longer binding on Americans' customs. When talking about this issue, American ethicists have said this: "Although we still live in a society where Christianity is the main religion, our personal morality is first of all to resist Christian morality. American society has not Re-accepting Christianity's morality about sexual life. Divorce has been fully recognized, and the freedom of sexual life between young men and women is fully accepted."

During the Second World War and its post-war period, American religious groups have grown significantly. The war pulled millions of American families into a Christian church or synagogue and prayed for the return of their loved ones on the front. The horror of war and the loss of confidence in the future have driven millions of people into religion to find refuge. After the end of the 1950s, this religious belief boom was greatly reduced. The growth rate of church members has stabilized. In the 1960s and 1970s, the percentage of church members to the total population remained steadily at 63%.

Since the 1970s, there has been a new religious fanaticism among some American youths. They often wear long shawls, rosary beads, and study the Bible: engaging in evangelism and inventing gospel rock music. Perhaps influenced by this group of people, the current churches in the United States have produced new forms of religious worship. Many churches have used socially popular jazz, rock, modern dance, contemporary art and folk music, folk dances, poetry, drama, slides and movies. These new rituals have angered some traditionalists. Once a parishioner had seen the band playing in his church, he asked the pastor indignantly: "Where do you think this is? Nightclub?" But many believers are enthusiastic about this new change, because this way They don't need to listen to the pastors for a long time in the church, and they don't have to listen to the old music of centuries ago.

www.richardtong.com.au

WHAT US MUST CONTAIN CHINA?
CHARLES CRAWHEIMER

If the ambassador is a person who is sent abroad to lie for the benefit of his country, then the politician can be said to be a person who lies for his own benefit in a domestic comfortable environment. American politicians have said that they have made a lie on how to deal with China. Assistant Secretary of State Winston Lord strongly denied that the United States is trying to contain China as she did in the Soviet Union. He insisted that our policy toward China is to engage policy rather than contain policy. Although Newt Gingrich's "National" TV show claimed that we should help the Chinese people to weaken their government, he then went on to say that his true intentions were not to weaken China at all.

What does this say is just a diplomatic lie? Because in the face of an emerging and aggressive China, any reasonable policy must include the following two parts: 1) to contain her when China spares no effort to expand outward, and 2) to weaken China, although it is a fake Marx. But it still implements an authoritarian regime that is ruthless. It is inconvenient for responsible politicians to tell the truth, but political commentators have no such scruples.

Does the containment policy mean the second cold war, and today's China plays the role of the old Soviet Union? The answer is not exactly like this. Because this battle between China and the United States does not include ideological factors. Old days The Soviet Union continued to have an ideological appeal until its death, and there were her sympathizers around the world. Today, China has different China from the Mao era, and she has no appeal in this regard. Today China is more of an old-style authoritarian regime. This regime does not bear the mission of the Savior. Her only goal is to gain power. Today, China is more like Germany in the late 19th century. It is a country that is rapidly growing stronger and therefore feels unable to continue to expand without expanding outward. China's neighbors have begun to feel this pressure. China is extending her tentacles to the depths of the South China Sea, claiming sovereignty over the South China Sea Islands hundreds of miles away from China; these islands are close to China's four neighboring countries, but they are China's rapidly powerful military powers. A place that can be reached. Indeed, when Russian and Western defense spending has been cut, China's defense spending has increased sharply, doubling in the past decade. The increased spending is being used to develop intercontinental missiles, more mobile Army and ocean-going navies.

China is not only deploying her newly acquired military power to the country, she is also exporting missiles and nuclear technology to countries like Pakistan and Iran. The alliance with Pakistan is to contain China's traditional enemy India from the flanks; and to meet with Iran is to serve as a pawn who is constantly making trouble for the former colonial masters.

To contain such a demon, you must start to act when its wings are not full. This containment policy means developing relations with China's neighbors, and Vietnam should be our starting point. There are extremely complex emotional disputes surrounding the restoration of relations with Vietnam, but the significance of restoring relations with Vietnam is completely geopolitical: Vietnam is a traditional enemy of China (they were short-lived in 1979) Border conflict). Therefore, we must make Vietnam our friend. Standing on a map, you can easily see the rest of the containment strategy: 1) establish a new security relationship with the democratic India, which has been liberated from the Cold War alliance maintained with the former Soviet Union; 2) reconstruction The US-Japan alliance, because the Clinton administration has recklessly forced Tokyo to buy American vaporizers, the alliance is currently under threat. This rash move directly shakes the cornerstone of our Pacific security system; 3) it is good with the Russians, regardless of them. In other respects, we have conflicts with us. Our interests are common in the fight against China.

The containment policy is not a cold war invention. It has been a fundamental principle of power politics for centuries. After the Napoleonic Wars, the Vienna Conference established France to curb too much vitality. In our time, the Atlantic Alliance has curbed the aggression of the Soviet Union. Between the two, the West has not been able to effectively contain the booming Germany. The result is two world wars. Faced with China's rising 21st century giant, we cannot let the historical tragedy repeat itself. But it is not enough to contain China alone. More importantly, Mr. Gingrich felt that he could not elaborate on it in detail: weakening China's fierce and aggressive totalitarian regime. This kind of weakening action can begin with unwavering support for dissidents like Wu Hongda. Because of his work on human rights, Wu Hongda is currently being held in China for theft of intelligence. This kind of support is self-evident in moral harmony. In addition to this, there is more political rationality. Yes, the United States succeeded in containing the Soviet Union, but the Soviet system was internally destroyed by dissidents like Solzhenitsyn, Shakhalinski and Sakharov. Wu and the thousands of dissidents he represents are the greatest threat to China's totalitarian rule. This is why the Chinese government has to deal with him at all costs. It is also why we must firmly support him.

Economic sanctions will not work. The use of economic sanctions against the fragile Soviet economy did not work in the past. Today, using economic sanctions to deal with the booming Chinese economy will not work. The best way is to launch a human rights war on the public stage. Boycotting Beijing to host the 2000 Olympic Games is a successful battle. Preventing China from joining the World Trade Organization on its own terms is another successful battle. Regimes like China are eager to gain legitimacy through the organization of such events. Our boycott is to convey an accurate message to them: liberalization or self-sufficiency in the international community. These benefits, which are good for improving the public image, can only be exchanged for progress in tolerance and democratization, which should be a guiding principle of our policy.

The implementation of the containment policy is aimed at preventing war. But the emergence of a tolerant and democratic regime on China's land will be a more reliable guarantee of peace. The time is needed to adopt a containment policy, and we should act and stick to it.

www.richardtong.com.au

SINO-US JOINT COMMUNIQUÉ, 1972 (FEBRUARY 28)

At the invitation of Premier Zhou Enlai of the People's Republic of China, the President of the United States of America, Richard Nixon, visited the People's Republic of China from February 21 to February 28, 1972. Accompanying the President were Mrs. Nixon, US Secretary of State William Rogers, Presidential Assistant Dr. Henry Kissinger and other US officials.

President Nixon met with Mao Zedong, chairman of the Communist Party of China, on February 21. The two leaders exchanged views earnestly and frankly on Sino-US relations and international affairs.

During the visit, President Nixon and Premier Zhou Enlai conducted extensive, serious and frank discussions on the normalization of relations between the United States of America and the People's Republic of China and other issues of mutual concern. In addition, Secretary of State William Rogers and Foreign Minister Ji Pengfei also held talks in the same spirit.

President Nixon and his party visited Beijing, visited cultural, industrial and agricultural projects, and visited Hangzhou and Shanghai, where they continued discussions with Chinese leaders and visited similar projects.

After the leaders of the People's Republic of China and the United States of America have not been in contact for so many years, they now have the opportunity to introduce each other's views on various issues frankly. The two sides believe that it is beneficial. They reviewed the international situation that experienced major changes and great turmoil and clarified their respective positions and attitudes.

The Chinese side stated: Where there is oppression, there is resistance. The country must be independent, the nation must be liberated, and the people want revolution. It has become an irresistible historical trend. Countries, big or small, should be equal, big countries should not bully small countries, and strong countries should not bully weak countries. China will never be a superpower and will oppose any hegemonism and power politics. The Chinese side expressed its strong support for the struggle of all oppressed and oppressed nations for freedom and liberation; the people of all countries have the right to choose their own social system in accordance with their own wishes, to safeguard their independence, sovereignty and territorial integrity, and to oppose foreign aggression. , interference, control and subversion. All foreign troops should be withdrawn to their home countries. The Chinese side expressed its firm support for the efforts of the people of Vietnam, Laos and Cambodia to achieve their goals. They firmly support the seven-point proposal of the Republic of South Korea's temporary revolutionary government and the explanation of two key issues in February this year and Indochina. Joint statement of the people's summit meeting; resolutely support the eight-point plan of the DPRK's peaceful reunification proposed by the government of the Democratic People's Republic of Korea on April 12, 1971 and the abolition of the "United Nations Korea Unification Council"; resolutely oppose Japan The resurrection and external expansion of militarism firmly supports the Japanese people's desire to establish an independent, democratic, peaceful and neutral Japan; they firmly advocate that India and Pakistan immediately withdraw their entire army to the country in accordance with the UN resolution on India and Pakistan. The respective parties in the territory and the Jammu and Kashmir ceasefire line firmly support the Pakistani government and people in the struggle for independence and sovereignty and the struggle of the people of Jammu and Kashmir for self-determination.

The United States stated that for peace in Asia and the world, efforts are needed to ease the current tensions and eliminate the basic causes of conflict.

The United States will work to establish a just and stable peace. This peace is just because it meets the aspirations of peoples and nations for freedom and progress. This peace is stable because it eliminates the danger of foreign aggression. The United States supports people all over the world in achieving personal freedom and social progress without external pressure and intervention. The United States believes that improving the links between countries with different ideologies in order to reduce the risk of confrontation caused by accidents, miscalculations or misunderstandings can help to ease tensions. Countries should respect each other and be willing to conduct peaceful competitions and let the actions make final judgments. No country should claim to be consistent and correct, and all countries must be prepared to re-examine their attitudes for the common good. The United States emphasizes that the people of Indochina should be allowed to decide their own destiny without foreign interference; the primary goal of the United States is to negotiate settlement; the Republic of Vietnam and the United States put forward eight on January 27, 1972. The point proposal provides the basis for achieving this goal; when the negotiations are not resolved, the United States expects to eventually withdraw all US troops from the region in line with the goal of self-determination in each country of Indochina. The United States will maintain its close ties and support for the Republic of Korea; the United States will support the efforts of the Republic of Korea to seek to ease tensions and increase ties on the Korean peninsula. The United States highly values the friendly relations with Japan and will continue to develop existing tight bonds. In accordance with the resolution of the UN Security Council on December 21, 1971, the United States endorsed the continuation of the ceasefire between India and Pakistan and the withdrawal of all military forces into the territory of the country and the respective ceasefire lines in Jammu and Kashmir. One side; the United States supports the rights of the peoples of South Asia to build their own future peacefully and without military threats, without making this region a target for competition among big powers. The social and foreign policies of China and the United States are essentially different. However, the two sides agree that regardless of the social system, all countries should deal with the relationship between countries based on the principle of respecting the sovereignty and territorial integrity of nations, non-infringement of other countries, non-interference in other countries' internal affairs, equality and mutual benefit, and peaceful coexistence. International disputes should be resolved on this basis without resorting to the threat of force and force. The United States and the People's Republic of China are prepared to implement these principles in their mutual relations.

SINO-US JOINT COMMUNIQUÉ, 1972 (FEBRUARY 28)

Taking into account the above principles of international relations, the parties declare that:

The normalization of Sino-US relations is in the interest of all countries;

Both sides hope to reduce the danger of international military conflicts;

Neither party should seek hegemony in the Asia-Pacific region, and each party opposes the efforts of any other country or group of countries to establish such hegemony;

Neither party is prepared to negotiate on behalf of any third party, nor is it prepared to reach an agreement or understanding with respect to other countries.

Both sides believe that any big country colluding with another big country against other countries, or the big country divides the scope of interests in the world, is contrary to the interests of the people of the world.

The two sides reviewed the long-standing serious disputes between China and the United States. The Chinese side reiterated its position: the Taiwan issue is a key issue that hinders the normalization of Sino-US relations; the government of the People's Republic of China is the sole legal government of China; Taiwan is a province of China and has already returned to the motherland; the liberation of Taiwan is China's internal affairs. Other countries have no right to interfere; all US armed forces and military facilities must be withdrawn from Taiwan. The Chinese government resolutely opposes any activities aimed at creating "one China, one Taiwan", "one China, two governments", "two Chinas", "Taiwan independence" and advocating "the status of Taiwan is undecided".

The US side stated that the United States recognizes that all Chinese on both sides of the Taiwan Strait believe that there is only one China and Taiwan is a part of China. The US government does not object to this position. It reiterated its concern for the peaceful resolution of the Taiwan issue by the Chinese themselves. With this prospect in mind, it recognizes the ultimate goal of withdrawing all US armed forces and military installations from Taiwan. In the meantime, it will gradually reduce its armed forces and military facilities in Taiwan as the tension in the region eases.

The two sides agree that it is advisable to expand the understanding between the two peoples. For this purpose, they discussed specific areas of science, technology, culture, sports and journalism, where the connection and exchange of people between them would be mutually beneficial. Both parties pledged to facilitate the further development of such contacts and exchanges. The two sides regard bilateral trade as another area that can bring mutual benefits and agree that equal and mutually beneficial economic relations are in the interest of the two peoples. They agreed to facilitate the gradual development of trade between the two countries.

The two sides agreed that they will maintain contacts through different channels, including sending US high-level representatives from time to time to Beijing to conduct specific consultations on the normalization of relations between the two countries and continue to exchange views on issues of common concern.

The two sides hope that the outcome of this visit will open up new prospects for bilateral relations. The two sides believe that the normalization of relations between the two countries not only serves the interests of the Chinese and American people, but also contributes to easing tensions in Asia and the world.

President Nixon, Mrs. Nixon and the US side expressed their gratitude to the Government and people of the People's Republic of China for their polite hospitality.

www.richardtong.com.au

LOOKING AT THE FUTURE OF SINO-US RELATIONS FROM THE GLOBAL STRATEGY OF THE UNITED STATES

I. US global strategic goals

1. Goal

The global strategic goal of the United States is to maintain and strengthen its dominant position after the collapse of the Soviet Union. The fundamental goal of this status was interpreted by Huntington as "preventing the emergence of a regional power in the Eurasia that challenges a US hegemonic position." He was extended to the past and claimed that "the United States has fought two world wars and one cold war to achieve this goal." Regardless of whether the person has the suspicion of cutting the historical facts with arguments, it undoubtedly speaks the core and essence of the global strategic concept of the United States.

2. means and steps

Out of the painstaking efforts of the United States for decades, the rational use of the security of the European and European countries during the Cold War has been favorable to the United States, forming a NATO and US-Japan military alliance. After the collapse of the Soviet Union, the Cold War ended. The United States shifted the functions of the military alliance to serve the United States' global strategic goals and turned the Japanese and European countries into a forefront of US interests. The new concept of NATO, the new pointers of the United

States and Japan exemplify this transformation, making member states become the assistants of the United States to dominate the world.

This kind of auxiliary status has not been fully stabilized, so it has become the focus of the current US foreign policy. The biggest test of the stability of its status is that the European and Japanese countries have poor anti-nuclear strike capability (due to the small population density of the country), and they have deep fears about the prospect of a nuclear war when the US dominates the world. The solution of the United States is to establish military alliances and build various defensive interception systems with military technology as the backing. The outsourcing of programs such as TMD and NMD is based on this consideration. If the success rate of TMD interception is over 97%, then its allies can feel rest assured that the function of the alliance can be reflected in the will of the United States, and it will not be feared and strongly opposed by allies. At the same time, the United States has technological advantages in this field. The technology and product exports brought by TMD will also bring considerable economic benefits to the United States. If the plan is implemented smoothly, then the United States can achieve both strategic and economic benefits, commonly known as stripping two skins from a cow.

This is certainly not the whole of the strategic goals that the United States will achieve. Alliance cannot certainly achieve a unified world. The party is to gather forces to ensure the success of the cut and reduce the risk. The success of the cut can achieve its dominant position. The party is the same for the same strategic purpose.

3. China's position in the US global strategy

In the Cold War era, in order to cope with the aggressive strategic offensive of the Soviet Union, the United States achieved normalization of relations with China. This is not due to the goodwill arrangement of the so-called "old friends of the Chinese people", but to the actual needs of the Soviet Union. As Kissinger said, "If we don't go to Beijing, then we can't go to Moscow."

: Due to the disintegration of the Soviet Union, China's 20-year reform achieved certain results, and its comprehensive national strength has increased, which has fundamentally reversed the original situation.

China's GNP is nearly one trillion US dollars (excluding Hong Kong, Macao and Taiwan), ranking seventh in the world after the United States, Japan, Germany, France and Britain. It is the largest outside of NATO and Japan. Compared with other major regional powers, Russia and India are about 340 billion US dollars, and China's status has been highlighted by the emergence of water. Therefore, even without ideological differences, China naturally becomes the preferred target of US global strategic goals. This goal will never be fundamentally changed because the Chinese government has shown goodwill to the United States in its internal affairs and diplomacy.

Second, the Chinese government and the public should give up their fantasy

It is often mentioned that there are two parties in the US policy toward China. In fact, the fundamental difference between the two factions is not in the division between contact and friendship, friendship and unfriendliness. We must never forget that both parties are Americans, starting from the interests of the same United States. The distinction between political claims does not mean the difference in fundamental interests, but also the advantages and disadvantages of weighing the positive and negative relationship with China, and it is caused by the difference in cost-benefit and risk judgment. If some people think that China's strength is not bad, the government is stable and the attitude is firm, then this person must think that the cost of confronting China is high and not desirable, and advocates contact; vice versa. If one day the United States thinks that China can be easily taken down and the risk costs are small, then the mitigation facts will surely disappear, and China will be in danger of destroying the country.

Those who advocate easing with the United States are starting from the interests and needs of China, the benefits of not confronting the United States, and the extent of the confrontation. However, this matter is not something the Chinese government and people can choose. In fact, within the scope of China's fundamental interests, no matter how far it is, it is not enough to meet the appetite of the United States, to achieve its strategic goals, and to achieve a fundamental easing of Sino-US relations. I will give an example of two major issues.

1. Economic, trade, democracy and human rights issues

If one day China becomes an American-style democracy, private ownership dominates the domestic economy. Individuals believe that under this circumstance, the conflicts between China and the United States will be more and more superficial. Take economic and trade as an example. If China is democratized, the voice of the people is of course more easily reflected in the policies and actions of the government. For example, in the United States, there are more than one hundred anti-dumping investigations each year in the United States, about half of which are for Chinese products. In addition, Super 301 is often invoked to protect domestic products. In fact, China's Foreign Trade Law also has corresponding provisions. The substantial damage suffered by Chinese enterprises and the damage of monopoly prices are endless. The Chinese industry is not without a strong willingness to sanction US companies and products, but these have not been reflected in government actions in a timely manner. In order to maintain a good international environment, the government has not only pursued these issues, but has regularly organized large-scale procurement groups to go to the United States. In addition, in the procurement behavior of the Chinese government, as a developing country, there is no tilting measure for the national industry. Compared with Japan, the difference is obvious. These are unimaginable under the democratic system. There is no doubt that a democratic China will pay more attention to protecting its legitimate economic interests. From the perspective of the United States, some strategists have predicted this result, stating that "democratized China is likely to be an ultra-nationalist government." The extreme word can be described as a slogan. It has been shown that a democratic China will pay more attention to its own interests and will be more inclined to take more restrictive measures against the illegitimate interests of the United States. This is even more inconsistent with the interests of the Americans. Therefore, in the case of knowing that everyone is not 100% internationalists, according to the principle of consistent derogation, the word "extreme" is added before Chinese nationalism to show the difference.

Therefore, the human rights and democracy of the United States are just a matter of feeling that they should use some of the great sticks to suppress China. The heart does not want China's democratic progress and prosperity. Among the Chinese people, the biggest illusion about the United States is this. I believe that once China has achieved American-style democracy, the United States will be willing to live in peace with China. This is really a good wish of innocent wishful thinking.

If China suddenly disintegrates like the Soviet Union in the process of democratization, the country's strength is weak and split, which is in line with the strategic goals of the United States. India and Russia are likely to cross the border and become China's number one strategic rival. China's situation will improve, but China has no country at this time. But the prospect of China's split and thus weakening, even the unscrupulous Western strategists did not have much hope. The famous Chinese expert, McFarquard, wrote innocently: The Western population is similar to China, divided into more than 50 independent countries, but China has successfully restored its empire. Huntington is still willing to tell the truth: China's relationship with the United States is a fundamental power struggle, and even the conflicting factors of civilization are no longer mentioned, and it is even more inconsistent with democracy and human rights.

China's weakening and splitting is a national nationality that cannot be traded with the United States. Therefore, Sino-US relations have improved and eased. The ball is undoubtedly on the US side and not on the Chinese side. China cannot trade with the United States in these respects. It is not that China and the United States are facing a war immediately, although some US strategies call for a war to defeat China. However, the outbreak and timing of the war will depend on China's counterattack capability and the attitude of the US allies. Fundamentally speaking, the attitudes and reactions of the United States and its allies are closely related to China's counterattack capability. China's relations with the United States and its allies The ability to counterattack ultimately determines the risk of war and the psychological limits that can be withstood.

2. Alliance and weapon proliferation

China is a big country. Although it is still a poor country, it is a world-famous country in terms of size and population. In view of this, China's behavior in the global village has taken a responsible and rational attitude.

Since the expiration of the Sino-Soviet Treaty of Friendship, China has never had such a military alliance of any kind and degree with any region or country. This is not a partner that China has no alliance in the world. It is based on the factors of maintaining world peace and regional stability. It does not give other members of the global village a sense of insecurity and pressure. Imagine if China and the countries that are willing to form alliances with China form a targeted alliance, and the United States and its allies deploy TMD to enhance its military superiority. China and its allies will engage in nuclear proliferation to promote world military balance, and the world will not become more Smoke and suffocation (what new ideas and new pointers have ruined the world), I am afraid that everyone in Europe and America will be restless. This is the result of China's self-restraint and a major contribution to world peace. Western strategists, for the purpose of belittle China, use only one sentence: "China has a strong sense of central empire and has a low willingness to form alliances with other countries." This is a good intention to deliberately wipe out China. The Chinese are not stupid enough to learn from the lessons of the British "glorious isolation" of the last century.

On the world stage, China has always adopted a restrained attitude when it disagrees with other Western countries, especially the United States. In the United Nations vote, China's veto power is rarely cited in some major events in recent years. In fact, China has actually made it incomprehensible in some big problems. It is an indisputable fact that there are few effective chips when dealing with the United States.

On the issue of weapons proliferation, compared with the world's largest arms exporting country, China's behavior is very restrained compared with the act of breaking the military balance (such as TMD). Moreover, it is too modest and has reached a level that does not guarantee national security. Under the current situation, moderately selective nuclear proliferation is actually conducive to the world military balance. This is also an indisputable fact.

See, China's goodwill has been "ignored" by the United States. I am afraid that there will be smart people who feel that Chinese isolation is just as good.

Third, the basis of action in the United States and China's countermeasures

There are many people in the country who have recently proposed that the middle and low wars with the United States are hard to avoid. Like Sino-US relations, this is also a question that is not chosen by the Chinese government and the people. How the intensity of the war is actually determined by the US. Starting from the long-term strategy of TMD, NMD and the United States, low- and medium-degree wars cannot achieve the strategic goals of the United States, and what is the use of TMD and NMD construction? China's split and weakening and the destruction of the country can achieve the strategic goals of the United States. This is by no means an alarmist, and the Chinese should not be taken lightly.

Of course, this is not to say that China will soon face the great disaster of destroying the country. Whether this catastrophic consequence occurs and when it has occurred, the United States has not yet reached a state where it can be arbitrarily chosen. The attitude of its allies and China's counter-measures are the two most critical factors. First of all, from the perspective of the behavior of the United States, the implementation of this behavior requires the strong support of its allies, and at least it is not strongly opposed. Without the support of allies, and the attitude of Russia does not touch the bottom, the United States takes great risks, and this determination is not easy. The key to the support of the allies (or no objection) is to disarm nuclear terror, which is subject to the maturity and full deployment of TMD technology (such as interception success rate of over 97%, and its allies are protected by TMD), which may take 120 years.

Second, Russia's strategic interest lies in maintaining China's confrontation with the US at the front line. In this incident of the Federal Republic of Yugoslavia, Russia is extremely restrained and tolerant (or weak, which is far more than Mie's expectation, otherwise Mie will definitely surrender from the beginning), which is not only because of the interests of the region or the small war risk (For example, if Russia only needs to transport 100-200 PUM or other new air defense missiles 100---200, NATO air strikes will not be carried out in the end, and the ground warfare is not afraid.) The purpose is to show the enemy to the east and the east, to win the advantage for Russia. Strategic position. The destruction of China will inevitably lead to direct confrontation between Russia and the United States and its own isolation, which is objectively unfavorable to its strategic interests. Therefore, the Russian factor is a containment factor for US action.

Finally, apart from external factors, the most important factor that plays a decisive role is ourselves. If China's comprehensive national strength is rapidly improved and its military capabilities are enhanced, the risk and cost of launching war in the United States will rise, and it may force the United States to abandon its goal of monopolizing the world and eventually return to the track of peaceful coexistence with China, thereby bringing peace to the world. And tranquility. In this regard, the Chinese government should have long-term strategic arrangements and corresponding countermeasures, and now it is not necessary to choose the major ones.

1. Improvement of overall national strength

The improvement of comprehensive national strength is a fundamental measure that depends on the speed and duration of economic development. Although it is not a process that is subject to subjective operations, it is promising to spur the potential for economic development. At present, the main problem of the domestic economy is the drag on the inefficient operation of state-owned enterprises under the conditions of occupying most of the social resources. At the same time, the development of private enterprises is difficult to obtain effective support.

In fact, after 20 years of reform and development, China has made great progress in the economy. The market has a certain scale, human resources have been quite reserved, and funds have accumulated quite a lot (only resident savings have reached 5.92 trillion).), already have the favorable conditions for economic take-off, and now the most urgent is to resolve to solve the institutional problems of state-owned enterprises, encourage protection and vigorously support the development of private enterprises, create conditions to encourage and guide private investment (currently adopted various types of consumption promotion) The means violates the frugal tradition of the Chinese people and is destined to have no ideal effect). If there is a breakthrough in the above three aspects, then the Chinese economy should have a rapid development period. For example, it is entirely possible to achieve and maintain an annual growth rate of 10%--14%, which will mean 5-- The GNP has doubled in 7 years, and GNP is likely to approach or exceed 10 trillion US dollars in 20 years. If this goal can be achieved, the ability to ensure national security and maintain peace in the world will be greatly enhanced.

2. Focus on strengthening national defense investment

A comprehensive arms race is not advisable.

The sum of the GNP of the US and Japan is close to 15 trillion US dollars. If the other NATO countries GNP is close to 25 trillion US dollars, the Chinese GNP is only 1 trillion US dollars, the economic strength is so wide, and the comprehensive arms race will drag. The Chinese economy has enabled the United States to achieve its goal of defeating the war. After the disintegration of the Soviet Union, some strategists in the United States attributed it to the United States' dragging the Soviet Union into an arms race that could not reach the Soviet Union's economy, causing economic setbacks to eventually lead to economic setbacks. Political disintegration). It is one of the sinister intentions of the US "mistaken bombing" of the US Embassy. It is no different from the Zhongji if China embarks on this path.

In the case that a comprehensive arms race is not advisable, a targeted breakthrough should be selected. From the current strategic arrangement of the United States, while maintaining its conventional maintenance advantages, it will focus on strengthening its strategic weapons defense capabilities (such as TMD) to enhance its overall advantages and minimize the risk and cost of war for itself and its allies. If this goal is achieved, the United States can solve the "basic power struggle between China and the United States" by following the prescriptions of some American strategists and "striving a war to defeat China". From this perspective, TMD is essentially a war preparation for China. Given China's size and population, conventional warfare cannot achieve the strategic goals of the United States once and for all. The United States is actually preparing for the nuclear war.

From the inside of the TMD system, spy satellites all over the world are the eyes of the system, and the integrated system of various communication means is its nerve. This is the two weaknesses of the system's vulnerability. Spy satellites and other military satellites are more desirable targets based on operability that is easy to distinguish and identify. Therefore, the development of anti-satellite weapons is a priority. It is clear that my Government and relevant departments have recognized this point, and my Disarmament Ambassador has requested in Geneva to place arms limitation in outer space on the negotiating agenda, hoping to partially resolve this issue through peaceful means. Obviously, the peaceful way cannot completely solve this problem, and developing effective counter-measures is the fundamental solution. Dispelling the eyes of the TMD system can only partially or completely reduce its effectiveness, such as using a laser weapon to completely destroy the system's spy and navigation satellites in a short period of time (such as a few hours). But what's more important is that there is no guarantee that it will be one step ahead of time, and it is difficult to make a preemptive strike in realistic choice. Therefore, the survival of strategic deterrent weapons and the improvement of penetration capabilities are equally important. A deterrent arsenal of considerable quantity and quality is indispensable.

3. Limitations of foreign policy

Many people start from good wishes and think that China should maintain a good relationship with the United States. It is not known that this alone cannot be done by China's efforts. It should be noted that the biggest obstacle for China to realize its global hegemony has accelerated the pace of the containment of me. The new US and Japanese indicators, the new agreement between the United States and the Philippines, and the new performance of Taiwan independence have the same internal relationship.

Foreign policy may be able to achieve certain national interests, but it seems powerless in the long-term realization of national interests. The realization of national security and major strategic interests will ultimately depend on national defense strength and comprehensive national strength (that is, the rich and powerful soldiers often referred to by the ancients). It is often said that the "weak country has no diplomacy" is the reason, the national strength is lacking, that is, it is difficult to apply its skills if there is a better strategy, and it is difficult to succeed in the joint failure. Therefore, the use of policies and strategies has its inherent limitations and cannot be expected to rely on it to achieve long-term goals. It is even better not to start from the good wishes of goodness, otherwise it will be subject to rejection and emotional damage again and again. If there are too many concessions due to diplomatic needs, it is even more harmful.

4. The timing of the Taiwan issue

The Taiwan issue has always been a fundamental issue between China and the United States. The United States hopes that Taiwan will become a "never-sinking aircraft carrier" during the war (McArthur's first creation), and will remain separated from the mainland in peacetime so as not to form a synergy to make China's economy too fast and strong, and to be a forever chip in diplomacy (just like playing chess in the next game) The same is true of the looting of materials, and the sense of distrust between the two sides will bring practical benefits to US arms dealers. Therefore, on this issue, the United States has been hesitant for seven years from the publication of the 72-year Shanghai Communique to the acceptance of the conditions for the establishment of diplomatic relations with Taiwan in 2007. I would like to draw the attention of the people here: The United States is not willing to accept it after thinking about it. Instead, it is too poor to cope with the offensive strategy of the Soviet big brother. It requires the strength of China to counter the Soviet Union. This is what it is.

After the disintegration of the Soviet Union, according to some American strategists, the "Chinese card" became worthless. The relationship between the United States and Taiwan and the support for Taiwan independence have also warmed up year by year, which should be better understood. This can also be well documented from the United States' deliberate deterioration of bilateral relations.

The reunification of the motherland is the fundamental interest of the entire Chinese nation and cannot be challenged. The root causes of the Taiwan independence forces are difficult to eradicate by the usual means. Li Deng's demise can not be fundamentally changed. The means of war is the last helpless choice.

In terms of time to resolve, it is difficult to have a leap in China's national strength and military strength, and it seems that it is too late to grasp the timing. Early resolution may help reduce the intensity of war and the depth of US involvement (after all, its TMD is not yet mature and deployed, and new pointers are especially unverified).

www.richardtong.com.au

A COMPREHENSIVE VIEW OF SINO-US RELATIONS

Just as Americans have various views and countermeasures on China, Chinese people, especially among scholars, also have many different viewpoints and policy recommendations. The previous year, Jiang Zemin visited the United States and Clinton to reach a "constructive strategic partnership" between China and the United States. The agreement, and then Clinton returned to China without going to Japan, so that a few Chinese scholars have been too optimistic about Sino-US relations. Some even wrote in the Hong Kong newspaper that the security issue in the Asia-Pacific region will be "China and the United States have the final say." After the US missile bombing of the Chinese Embassy in Yugoslavia last May, a few Chinese scholars believed that the opposite side of Sino-US relations was the main one. Some even believed that there was only a "negative cooperative relationship" between China and the United States. Guided by "structural contradictions" in Sino-US relations. The commentator stated that the so-called "structural contradiction" refers to the fact that the United States wants to maintain its hegemonic status in the 21st century, and China, whose comprehensive national strength is growing rapidly, is the country most likely to challenge the hegemonic position of the United States. The modern version of the Warring States hegemony concept of "structural contradictions" makes people feel like they have met before. For the time being, this is almost the same as the arguments put forward by the politicians and the media that the United States advocates a containment policy against China. The only difference is that they are not generalized with concepts such as "structurality."

The arguments constructed by the opposing parties for their respective countermeasures are actually in the same vein, which is really intriguing! If we put time into China's Warring States era, we can find that this "structural contradiction" is in line with the dominance of the princes who sought to establish their status at that time. The overlord of the Warring States era was most concerned with how to suppress and destroy all potential hegemonic challengers. Therefore, it may be said that this view is a modern version of the theory of international relations in the Warring States period. However, the times have changed after all, and modern international relations have become more complicated than ancient international relations. The old simplistic concept of hegemony clearly does not apply to contemporary international relations. Don't simplify the "structural" factors. When observing the post-Cold War international relations, there are two major trends that should not be ignored: First, the rapid development of world economic integration and globalization, and the corresponding inter-state and region. The deepening of interdependence; and second, the growing global importance of human survival and security, including environmental protection, the proliferation of weapons of mass destruction, serious terrorist activities, drugs Trading and refugee flows, etc. No matter from what angle, including the observation of contemporary international relations from the perspective of so-called "structurality", it is reasonable to take these two major trends into consideration. Otherwise, it will be incomplete and incomplete. Therefore, when studying Sino-US relations, it is obviously one-sided if we only pay attention to the possible impacts and negative impacts of the changes in the overall national strength of China and the United States. The reason why the late American most prestigious Chinese Tong Bao Da can and still be active in other mainstream Chinese scholars such as Osenberg, He Hanli, etc., is worthy of praise, mainly because they see the existence of national interests between China and the United States. At the same time of the conflict, it was able to remind the US government and the media with keenness. During the post-Cold War era, China and the United States had vital common interests in these two major trends.

The United States is the world's most developed economy and technology, while China is the largest developing country with the largest potential market. There is huge economic complementarity between China and the United States. At the same time, when solving the above-mentioned global problems, the United States cannot do without China's cooperation. All of this is an obvious fact and a "structural" factor that will work for a long time. It should be seen that this is a real and objective basis for cooperation between China and the United States. The cooperation between China and the United States on this basis is constructive and enthusiasm, and should never be labeled as a "negative" hat.

The United States does not "ignite"

Of course, we should not naively believe that under any circumstances, China and the United States will never have another military conflict or even a war. The biggest friction between China and the United States is on the Taiwan issue. Moreover, in the foreseeable future, this is also the only problem that may lead to military conflict between the two countries. However, considering various factors, this possibility is not large. The main reasons are: 1. Regardless of whether it is on Taiwan or internationally, it has been widely recognized that Chinese leaders must be forced to use force if the Taiwan authorities publicly declare independence or amend the law through constitutional amendments. The warning is true. The vast majority of the people on the island are worried about the war between the two sides of the strait. It is generally hoped to maintain the status quo. The people's heart is so, even the president of the Democratic Progressive Party, Chen Shui-bian, has to lower the tone of the Taiwan independence. 2. It is not in the national interest of the United States to fight with China because of the Taiwan issue. It will disrupt its global strategic layout and violate the "cost and benefit" balance that Americans have always regarded as the standard. in principle. 3. In terms of politics, the basic US policy goal toward China is still "peaceful evolution." Taiwan is a pawn to implement this policy. Maintaining peace in the Taiwan Strait and Taiwan's "unification and independence" is most conducive to its role.

The final direction of Taiwan's reunification or independence depends to a large extent on the political evolution of the island. However, if the United States unwisely continues to take some serious measures that objectively encourage Taiwan's separatist forces, such as substantially increasing the arms sales of high-tech equipment, and even integrating Taiwan into the theater missile defense system (TMD), the US and Taiwan are actually formed. Military alliances, then leaders like Lee Teng-hui in Taiwan are likely to take risks and the United States may be dragged into a cross-strait war that they are involved in.

www.richardtong.com.au

CHINA AND THE UNITED STATES SHOULD KNOW EACH OTHER MORE

Dr. Jia Hao, director of the Washington China Studies Center, believes that the US as a superpower is adopting policies to deal with and deal with the rising China. How China is the largest developing country, how to recognize today's The structure of international relations dominated by the United States to a large extent is the biggest contradiction between China and the United States.

The three-day large-scale international seminar on "The Challenges of China and Sustainable Development in the 21st Century" held a "China-US Relations in the 21st Century" report meeting this morning. Jia Hao and Dr. Min Minxin, Senior Research Fellow at Carnegie Institute for International Peace, Dr. Hong Zhaohui, Associate Professor of Safenga State University, and Dr. Xu Deqing, Visiting Research Fellow at Yale University, respectively expressed their views on Sino-US relations.

Jia Hao said that the core and foundation of Sino-US relations are different. The views of the two sides are different. The Chinese side believes that the relations between China and the United States affect the stability of the Asia-Pacific region and even the world; the two sides should seek common ground while reserving differences on weapons proliferation, economic cooperation and human rights. The most important issue between the two countries is the Taiwan issue. What does the US think? Similarly, the US side also believes that the Taiwan issue is the most sensitive issue and may even lead to catastrophic military conflict. Most American politicians do not want China to surpass the United States in a short period of time, or China becomes a superpower; most US officials are adopting or willing to adopt a "communication" policy toward China. Of course, there are some people in the United

States who are trying to "westernize and divide China", but this is not the core of US government policy.

Dr. Xu Deqing believes that the United States is adopting a policy of contact and preparedness against China. Contact, I hope to introduce China into the international system - it is currently dominated by the United States; it is prepared to worry about China's "demonization" and attempts to contain China. But no matter what kind of policy is adopted, the United States should respect China and be inclusive to treat Chinese culture or Eastern culture. At the same time, the United States should look at China from the perspective of China's history. Especially on the Taiwan issue, we must fully understand China's sovereignty. A strong position on the issue, fully understand China's "heartache" and "historical scars."

Xu Deqing said that China and the United States are the most important bilateral relations in world affairs, but at present they are not allies, not confrontational or non-competitive. The two countries should not place too much emphasis on ideology in their exchanges. The relations between the two countries should not be influenced by their own politics. The United States should pay particular attention to it. At the same time, the two countries should have normal channels of communication.

Dr. Minxin Min pointed out that the Republican Party's Cold War consciousness is much stronger than that of the Democratic Party. The rise of the Republican Party has a great influence on China's policies in Congress, and the Republican Party's hatred against Clinton has turned into a hatred against China policy. He said that after the Cold War, the non-governmental forces in the United States have been strengthened. For example, human rights groups and labor organizations are often politicized on some issues. The US media has not changed its impression of China since 1989.

Min Minxin believes that China must pay attention to these factors in dealing with the United States.

CHINA AND THE UNITED STATES SHOULD KNOW EACH OTHER MORE

www.richardtong.com.au

US MILITARY

THE UNITED STATES WILL UPDATE SIX THOUSAND NUCLEAR WARHEADS

The US Department of Energy will renovate more than 6,000 aging nuclear warheads in the next fifteen years, but the plan has been severely criticized by arms control supporters.

The number of plans to renovate 6,000 warheads is nearly double the number of deployables under the START II Treaty. Department of Energy officials said the additional warheads were "non-active reserves" -- about 2,500 to 3,000 refurbished warheads could allow US nuclear capabilities to suddenly produce additional warheads against other countries.

However, the plan was attacked by advocates of arms control, who asserted that there were too many 6,000 warheads stored - especially as the United States was trying to convince India, Pakistan, North Korea and other countries to cut their nuclear weapons programs.

Nolan, director of the International Program of the Century Fund, said that the president talked about the dangers of nuclear weapons. The technicians of the national laboratories refurbished a large number of reserve weapons. However, the scale of the renovation was not affected by any agreement or treaty.

However, the Defense Ministry official responsible for strategic weapons insisted that the United States Duma should delay the signing of the Second Stage Strategic Arms Reduction Treaty, and the United States must prepare for the overthrow of the agreement.

The official pointed out to the Washington Post that the United States could also cut additional warheads after the treaty came into force.

Both Russia and the United States have reduced the number of reserve weapons in accordance with the level set by the START II Treaty; but the US Congress has banned the deployment of US military warships to less than 6,000, until Moscow signed the Second Strategic Arms Reduction Treaty. "until. The US Senate signed the Second Stage Strategic Arms Reduction Treaty in 1996.

According to the report, the United States spends about $4.6 billion a year on nuclear weapons.

www.richardtong.com.au

AEGIS-CLASS GUIDED MISSILE DESTROYER

The United States has agreed to sell four "Aegis"-class guided missile destroyers to Taiwan. Because this type of warship has strong anti-missile capabilities, it has always been one of Taiwan's coveted weapons.

As early as in the past few years, Taiwan has built docking facilities and related logistics support equipment specially built for this type of warship. The "King Kong" class guided missile destroyers of Asian countries and Japan are also equipped with the "Aegis" system of the United States.

The United States has decided to sell four sets of "Aegis" systems in Taiwan. Although it cannot guarantee that Taiwan will not be attacked by mainland missiles, it will be beneficial to complete the early warning capability of the "Aegis" system and the availability of the US satellite early warning system in the future. The Taiwanese theater missile defense system, therefore, the United States agreed to sell the "Aegis" system, which is equivalent to the entry of the "Treasure Missile Defense System" (TMD).

According to Taiwan media reports, the Taiwan Defense Ministry's Staff Headquarters proposed the forces needed for the missile defense system in the Taiwan-Taiwan region to address the threat of the mainland missile, including the "war zone high-area defense system" to protect urban security, and the "patriots to defend important institutions and facilities." "Flying missile defense system", "protective force station, large-scale outer (detached) island defense system security "military air defense missile system", and "Navy low-level defense network system" to protect Taiwan's external navigation channel safety.

The "Aegis" combat system is the most important part of the naval low-level defense network system architecture. "Aegis" system AEGIS is an abbreviation of five English words in the early stage of aerial early warning. In Greek mythology, AEGIS is the "shield" used by the gods Zeus and Athena, which also explains the main functions of the Aegis system. It is in defense.

The US "Aegis" class ship costs about one billion dollars. It is equipped with a standard type II air defense missile to intercept incoming missiles or aircraft at sea. The "Aegis" class ships are equipped with a total of ninety-nine standard two-type missiles, twenty in the front cabin and sixty in the rear cabin. Taiwan's successful class ships are only equipped with forty standard one-type missiles.

The soul of the "Aegis" combat system is the radar antenna on the left and right sides below the Aegis ship bridge. The AN-SPY-1 phase array radar, with a high power wave of 4 megawatts, continuously scans three hundred and sixty degrees. Space, and simultaneously tracking hundreds of targets, with the ship's fire control system, can filter out missiles or aircraft that are attacking hundreds of kilometers away in about ten seconds, depending on their speed, altitude, type and possible Carry weapons and handle up to three hundred threatening targets.

www.richardtong.com.au

AMERICAN ELECTRIC STEALTH DESTROYER

The US Navy recently announced plans to use revolutionary all-electric technology to develop a new generation of warships that dominate the world. The DD-21 destroyer, which was built with this technology, can save up to 500 missiles due to space saving and greatly reduced noise and exhaust emissions. The "invisible" capability is also greatly enhanced, reducing the chances of being discovered by the enemy.

US Secretary of the Navy Danzick said that the Ministry of National Defense will submit a budget to Congress at the beginning of next month, suggesting that it should allocate US$250 million (about HK$1.95 billion) to develop a set for the next six years. The DD-21 destroyer's "electric propulsion technology", and this technology may be used in all surface ships, or even submarines. Danzik said the Navy plans to spend $25 billion (about 195 billion Hong Kong dollars) to build thirty-two DD-21 destroyers. It is expected that the first ship will be in service after ten years.

Equivalent to the sea missile launch pad

The DD-21 destroyer is a ground attack type warship. Two heavy artillery pieces will be installed on the ship. The platform stern part can be vertically assembled with up to five hundred different types of missiles, including the powerful Tomahawk cruise missile. The launch attack is like a sea missile launch pad; in addition to the effectiveness of the sea defence, it can also provide fire support to the amphibious or ground forces. In addition, the DD-21 also has functions such as command, monitoring, intelligence gathering, and non-combat operations. Unlike current warships, the destroyer does not use reduction gears and drive shafts to control the propellers, but instead uses an engine (gas turbine or diesel engine) to propel smaller, quieter and more efficient generators. The motor connected to the generator is used to control the propeller, which can be easily rotated. Moreover, the entire ship only needs one engine, and it can simultaneously carry out the work of propelling ships and generating electricity.

The crew is reduced from 300 to 95

With this engine, the acceleration can be increased by at least 20 knots in two minutes. At the same time, due to the use of electricity, the chimney on board will no longer exist, reducing the chance of hit by infrared-guided anti-ship missiles. This design can also save a lot of space for warships, not only to expand the room of the soldiers on board, but also to install more advanced weapons, such as lasers and electronic weapons still under development. As the number of machines required is reduced, the number of staff can be reduced from the current three hundred to a maximum of ninety-five; there is no large reduction gear and drive shaft, which can avoid the enemy's discovery and smooth boat. Body, reduce the possibility of being locked by enemy radar. Danzik described this as a "transition of important moments", but it is not just a matter of changing the way forward. He said: "This "integrated power system" can make the ship more flexible in all aspects. These changes are revolutionary." The head of the Naval Surface Warfare Department, Mullen, described: "From the operational point of view, this It is a very important development."

www.richardtong.com.au

US 75TH RANGER

Among the many special warfare units in the United States, the Ranger (also known as the assault or special attack team) is an elite unit with a long history and strong military force. The Rangers with glorious history and excellent traditions carry out the role of the World Police in various places with unrespective spirit and perseverance, and gain international recognition and praise.

The basic upstream cavalry is a light infantry and has nothing to do with the cavalry. It can use a variety of vehicles to quickly enter the theater to perform missions, so often the chariots have completed the mission before other special forces arrive. Just like the motto "Rangers, lead the way" and the black beret and streamer armor with the RANGER lettering on behalf of the spirit of the Ranger, it has always been a symbol of the glory and dignity of the Ranger.

In the Second World War, the predecessor of the 75th Cavalry Regiment, the 5307th Mixed Detachment of the United States and the Chinese New Army jointly fought in the Burmese theater. Therefore, the left side of the Ranger emblem is the emblem of the Republic of China, the white star on the right symbolizes the star of Myanmar, and the lightning in the middle represents the Ranger. The speciality of the assault enemy, and the four colors of green, red, white and blue represent the four-color code used by the 5307 mixed detachment.

The origins of the Rangers can be traced back to the small army that used the Rangers name and tactics during the American colonial period in the 1670s. At that time, in order to cope with the Indians who were good at raid tactics, the United States formed a small detective team to patrol the area around the area to observe enemy activities and provide early warning. Because their patrol distance is called "Range", it is generally said that the soldiers of this team are "Ranger". The first regular Ranger unit was established in New Hampshire in 1756, and

Major Robert Rogers first organized the nine-game Rangers to represent the United Kingdom against France and the Indians. They widely used fast guerrilla and reconnaissance tactics to sneak into enemy targets, and the patrol distance was as high as 400 哩. The tradition of 19 Rangers creeds and black berets established by Major Rogers was formed at the time.

During the American Revolution, the local army established the Rangers, including the commando 'The Corps of Rangers, which was led by Daniel Morgan, who led a group of experienced infantry. And led by Francis Marion, repeatedly with Washington. The guerrillas "Swamp Fox", which fought side by side with the army, were not only trusted by Washington, but also impressed the British. Because of the independence of the United States, the Army had 12 consecutive Rangers.

The more famous Rangers of the Civil War were the cavalry led by Colonel John S. Mosby of the Southern Army. They used team tactics to quickly assault the Northern Army's outposts or important positions. Regardless of the Revolution and the Civil War, the US military has confirmed the importance of the Rangers to the war. The tactical and military ideology used at the time also formed the basis of today's cavalry combat guidelines.

Rangers during World War II

On May 26, 1942, during the Second World War in the European Theater, Major General Lucian K. Truscott wanted to establish a US military unit that could fight alongside the British commandos. In addition, in order to highlight the American characteristics, the unit was named " Ranger" and led by Major William O. Darby. On June 19, 942, the 1st Ranger Battalion was officially born in Northern Ireland. Most of the troops were from the 1st Armored Division and the 34th Infantry Division. They also received battlefield survival and amphibious landing training at the Scottish Commando Training Center. About a month later, 44 Rangers and 5 officers joined the Canadian and British commandos to participate in the Battle of Dieppe Raid, becoming the first US military to fight the Germans. After that, the battalion commander of the Lieutenant Colonel Darby led the Rangers Battalion into North Africa, performing infiltration and destruction tasks in Albania and Tunisia, and pioneering the infantry division. As a result of the brilliant results, not only the president's praise, but also the rangers were expanded to the sixth battalion. The 1st, 3rd, and 4th cavalry battalions combined with Army chemistry, engineering, and artillery units into the '6615 Ranger Force' and continued to be led by Darby. In 1943, 6615 Rangers troops had brilliant results in the Italian theater.

During the Second World War, the more famous battle of the Rangers was the 2nd and 5th battalions involved in the Norman Land. In 1944, the main force of D-Day's landing in Normandy was the 7th and 5th Legion of the US Army. The Rangers belonged to the 5th Corps. The 5th Army's main force is the 29th Infantry Division, the right wing is the 1st Infantry Division, and the left wing is the 'Provisional Ranger Group' consisting of the 2nd and 5th Rangers. The average person thinks that the American infantry of the Second World War is characterized by youth, high education, and generally lack of combat experience, but for the Rangers, the battlefield is where they play their talents. On the day of landing, the US military encountered a fierce attack from the German 352th Infantry Division. When other infantrymen were unable to advance by firepower, the highly trained Rangers quickly broke through the line of defense without fear of life and death. Although the casualties are extremely heavy, such as the preparation of the second camp C-70 of 70 people (the film rescues the background of Rennes soldiers), 58 people died after the landing and even the whole company was released. However, the heroic and good warfare of the Rangers not only made the 29th Division infantry fighting side by side look at each other, but also won the praise of General Norman D. Cota, the deputy division commander of the 29th Division, thus leaving the immortal wise saying "Ranger, lead the way" (Ranger, lead the way))!". After the war, six Rangers Battalions were also abolished.

The other lesser known rangers of the Second World War included the 29th Ranger Corps from the 29th Infantry Division and the 5307 Mixed Detachment of the Myanmar Theater codenamed "ERRILL'S MARAUDERS". The 5307 mixed detachment led by Brigadier General Frank D. Merrill was the US military detachment in the national army. It is cooperating with the new 38 division of the National Army led by General Sun Liren of China, as well as the new 22 divisions, the new 30 divisions and 50 divisions. They went deep into the jungles of Burma and repelled the 18th Division of the Japanese Army, which attempted to attack China from the southwest, leaving a glorious page in the history of the anti-Japanese war. The 5307 Mixed Detachment was reorganized into the 75th Infantry Regiment in 1954, the predecessor of the 75th Ranger.

Korean War

The biggest change in the Korean wartime cavalry was the ability to airborne, and the combat formation was very different from that during World War II. During the Second World War, the Rangers were independent fighters in each battalion. In the Korean War, each of the 112-member Rangers was assigned to the 18,000-man infantry division as the pioneer of each division. In the actions of the divisions, the cavalry is responsible for cover, detect, block or assault. In 1950, the Army appointed Colonel John Gibson Van Houten to select a group of Ranger candidates to train in Fort Bunning, Georgia, mostly from the 82nd Airborne Division. The training time is mostly carried out at night. The training subjects include light weapon operation, night skydiving, amphibious landing, blasting and fighting, etc., and each soldier must be familiar with Korean terrain. The first batch of trained 1st Rangers Airborne arrived in South Korea on December 17, 1950 and was incorporated into the 2nd Infantry Division. Immediately after the 2nd and 4th Rangers joined the theater, the 2nd Company was included in the 7th Infantry Division, and the 4th Company was under the jurisdiction of the 9th Army Department and the 1st Cavalry Division. From 1950 to 1951, the various Rangers joined the battlefield one after another. They used the amphibious methods of sea, land and air to penetrate the enemy's territory and continue to create glory. Among them, the 1st Ranger airborne was connected to the night airborne theater, and advanced through the front line to the enemy's back nine or more. The day and night assaulted the headquarters of the 12th Division of the North Korean Army, prompting the two regiments stationed in the area to panic and flee the scene. The 2nd and 4th Rangers' battlefields crossed the 38-degree line and directly hit Maoshan City on the border between China and South Korea. In addition, he was affiliated to the 24th Infantry Division. The 8th Ranger Airborne Company, known as the Devil's Company, even smashed the People's Volunteer Army with a small number of 33 people and searched for as many as 70 soldiers. The 8th company had only 2 deaths and 3 injuries. So taking advantage of the glorious tradition of 'Rangers, lead the way!' during the Second World War, the Rangers participating in the Korean War once again created a glorious new page in the history of the United States. But with the end of the Korean War, all the Rangers joined each other.

Vietnam War

The 75th Infantry Regiment with long-range reconnaissance capability was established in Okinawa in 1954 and was adapted from the 475th Infantry Regiment. The predecessor of the 475th Infantry Regiment was the 5403 mixed detachment that was famous during the Second World War. On February 1, 1969, the long-range investigation company from the nine infantry divisions and the Indiana National Defence Corps, who joined in Vietnam, transferred to the 75th Infantry Regiment to become the 13th Ranger. The Rangers of the Vietnam War were very different from the past, including the selection of the troops to be opened from the various units of the Army, and training in Vietnam. During the operation, each unit was divided into operational responsibility areas. From selection, training to combat, the grassroots leading cadres are unified and no longer controlled by the central high-level. Unlike the passive offensive of the general infantry, the Rangers often take the initiative of 6 people, 1 team or even 2 people. They use airdrops, helicopters to descend, or use vehicles, speedboats and walking to penetrate the enemy's back area. In addition to investigating enemy situations or assault operations, they penetrated the enemy zone to conduct damage assessments of the B-52 bomber during the 'Arc' bombing. Due to the excellent performance of the Rangers in the Vietnam War, the US Army Chief of Staff Creighton Abrams changed the 75th Infantry Regiment to the permanent 75th Ranger Corps and became the first permanent Ranger unit of the US Army.

change

In the American war history, the upper cavalry has always been a commando team born in response to the war, so with the end of the Vietnam War, the cavalry troops can not escape the fate of dissolution. However, in 1974, the Chief of Staff of the Army, General Creighton Abrams, believed that a permanent nature of the Rangers should be established in response to the changing international situation. The 1st and 2nd Rangers Battalion were established in Georgia, and the 1st Battalion was stationed at the Hunter Army Air Base in Georgia and the 2nd Battalion was located in Fort Lewis, Washington.

Iran 'Desert One' action

The incident occurred in the 1980 US Embassy in Tehran, the capital of Iran. The United States wanted to send troops to rescue the personnel in the embassy and called the operation Deserter One. The original plan was to be rescued by the Army's 1st Special Forces combat detachment, the famous Delta Force. The nine RH-53D sea-type horse-type helicopters carried US troops and embassy helicopters to the airport in eastern Tehran, so that all personnel could transfer to Iran by transport. The Rangers sent the 1st Ranger Battalion C, which is part of the 75th Infantry Regiment, to support. The mission was to clear the enemies in the airport to ensure the safety of the aircraft and personnel. The

Rangers received a modelling exercise in Egypt to cope with various emergencies, but I did not know whether the command was improper or the equipment was poorly maintained. On the eve of the action, two RH-53D helicopters collided in the air, and one helicopter suddenly broke down, which not only forced The early exposure of the action made the rescue mission even more difficult. Due to the exposure of the action, the enemy not only prepared for it, but also immediately dispersed the hostages to various regions, making this action forced to cancel. The C. C. and the Delta Forces, which have been on standby in Egypt, can only return to gloom.

Grenada "Urgent Fury" action

In 1983, the US military finally got rid of the shadow of the Vietnam War and greeted the first large-scale victory after the Vietnam War. The United States' military-fighting island is a means for the government authorities to temporarily mobilize in order to achieve certain political interests, and there is not enough preparation time for the US military. When the US military used a large number of heavy weapons to attack the Cuban army, they did not forget a group of American medical students in the saltwater blue campus. The Rangers not only joined the Army Rapid Deployment Force (RDF) attack, but also joined the action to save students. The first task of the Rangers was to occupy the salt water airport and the school district to allow the paratroopers of the 82nd Airborne Division to land smoothly, but the Scouts of the operation could not log in successfully to provide information.

On the morning of October 25th, the B Company of the 1st Ranger Battalion took the lead in airborne salt water to the airport. The landing cavalry members immediately encountered two Russian BTR-60PB armored vehicles and the Cuban army. However, with the support of the M67 shoulder-mounted recoilless gun and the AC-130H gunboat, the Rangers immediately destroyed the enemy armored vehicles and established fortifications. Immediately after the first battalion, the A company and the second battalion cavalry airborne and quickly cleared the enemy forces around the airport, and covered the 82nd Airborne Division successfully landed. Although there were successive attempts by the Cuban army to recapture the airport, they were all repelled by the firepower of the US military. Different from the mentality that the US military did not win in the Vietnam War, the political and operational goals of the US military's outstretched island were the same. Therefore, whenever a lightly loaded ranger encounters a powerful Cuban army, they will ask for gunboats to land or bomb in the air. When the jungle becomes a scorched earth, the soldiers will go to clean up the battlefield. But at the same time, the first battalion C-running cavalry who went to the Liqimeng Mountain Prison to rescue the hostages was not so lucky. Due to the misjudgment of intelligence, the UH-60 Black Hawk helicopter loaded with the Rangers was exposed to the enemy's anti-aircraft fire, and the helicopter was shot down without any air support. Other seriously damaged helicopters immediately withdrew and landed on nearby naval vessels. The second wave of rescue operations was successfully carried out with the support of the Marine Corps. The Rangers had the support of the AC-130H gunboat and the AH-1S Cobra helicopter. The 1st Battalion's Rangers took three CH-46 helicopters to rescue students from other areas. Upon arrival at the scene, the Rangers not only missed the landing point, but also one helicopter crashed into the tree and crashed, but the Rangers managed to rescue all the students.

The last mission of the Rangers on the island was on October 27th. The 2nd Battalion and the 1st Battalion C were ordered to attack the enemy training base near the airport. The troops traveled by four UH-60 helicopters, but one helicopter suddenly crashed and landed on two other helicopters during the landing. This accident not only caused the destruction of all three helicopters, but also caused the loss of 3 deaths and 4 injuries for the 2nd Battalion. However, the rest of the rangers easily occupied the base without the mission, because the enemy had already withdrawn from the area. Of course, the U.S. military's Oolong incident caused the shadow of the gondolier's glorious war history.

Panama "Just Cause" action

On October 3, 1984, the Rangers continued to add the 3rd Battalion to become a standing Ranger unit of the three battalions. In 1989, when the United States sent troops to Panama to arrest the strongman Norega's just invasion, the Rangers once again played a pioneering role. The 1st Battalion of the Rangers, the 3rd Battalion C Company and the regiment even the Golden Squad airborne at the Dorega International Airport and quickly advanced to the headquarters of the Panama City Occupational Defense Forces. On the other hand, the second battalion of the Rilhau Airport, the third battalion A, B, and the regiment even the black squad did not go so smoothly. They were violently attacked by the Panamanian Defence Forces. Although the Rangers quickly occupied the airport with the support of the AC-130 gunboat, five soldiers were killed. Immediately afterwards they raided the southern Panamanian Special Forces. Because the troops were on vacation, the Rangers easily captured the unit. After the occupation of Panama, the Rangers immediately took on the task of maintaining order and protecting the safety of public facilities. In 1990, the Rangers returned to the country with glory. In total, the operation lost a total of 5 deaths and 42 injuries, capturing 1,014 enemy troops and more than 18,000 weapons.

Wave Bay War

During the Bowan War, the 75th Range Cavalry Corps went to the Middle East to serve as the coalition reserve team. In the 1991 Desert Storm Operation, the 1st row of the A Ranger Battalion A and the Arrangement of the Weapons (Strengthening Row) and the C Company assisted the coalition rapid reaction force to assault the Iraqi military stronghold. The Tuan Tuan Company conducted a large-scale airborne exercise in Kuwait. Although the Rangers did not fully participate in the first-line battle, their strong combat power has a small deterrent effect on Iraq.

Somalia "Restore Hope" action

Between August and 10, 1993, the 3rd Battalion of the Rangers, B, formed a task force to travel to Somalia to support the United Nations Peace Forces. In addition to assisting the refugees, they also conducted seven missions to search for the guerrilla leader Aidid. The most fierce battle took place during the day of October 3. The Rangers and the Delta Special Forces jointly went to the capital of Mogadishu to attack the military elements to hunt Aidid. At the beginning of the operation, the special team members quickly subdued the enemy, but the helicopters stranded in the air attracted more enemy troops. As a result, two helicopters were shot down and many casualties were caused. The rest of the team was surrounded by the army and could not leave. Although the coalition forces launched four rescue operations one after another,

But they were all stubbornly resisted by the enemy. Until the evening, the coalition forces sent two additional task forces including the Seals and Rangers, two Malaysian mechanized companies, and one Pakistani tank and the Air Force special forces to rescue. After the fierce battle, the coalition finally rescued the besieged team members, but also paid a considerable price. In total, the Allied Coalition paid the price of 18 deaths and 80 injuries. The light cavalry itself had 16 deaths and 57 injuries and 1 loss. The failure of this action lies in the lack of control of intelligence and the rush to act during the day, which not only caused major casualties in the special operations forces, but also the shame of the team members being dragged to the city by the army. However, the sacrificial spirit of the Rangers has once again won unanimous praise from all over the world.

Ranger warrior in the trench

Selection and training

As early as during the Korean War, the Rangers had specialized training institutions. In addition to the establishment of the Ranger Training Department in the Army Infantry School, the Rangers also have exclusive training brigades and four Ranger Training Camps. In addition to developing long-distance surveillance (LRS) and infantry combat leaders and training the cavalry units, and training foreign soldiers and government personnel, including Chinese military officers who are trained in the United States. Unlike the Army Special Forces, the Rangers do not recruit female soldiers. Most of their troops are from volunteers from various units of the Army. Others are other services and foreign soldiers. Volunteers who participated in the selection first need to be physically and mentally healthy and have no bad records. After passing airborne training, they can participate in the selection of the cavalry. In the 10-week selection and training, the average elimination rate exceeded 60%. The process and contents are as follows:

1. Ranger basic training:

The candidates completed the check-in process at the Rogers camp in the Bunningham Ranges, Ga., and went to the Darby camp in the North Carolina forest for selection. In addition to the long-distance running, the selection content also needs to endure hunger and cold in a harsh environment, and the exhausted battlefield life experience is eliminated if it is unacceptable. Next is the important "Raval Caving Evaluation Phase (RAP)", whose selection and training subjects are as follows:

Army Physical Fitness Test:

Through Volley, stand up for 2 minutes and 52 seconds, sit-ups for 2 minutes and 62 seconds, and complete the 2nd running and horizontal bar 6 physical fitness test standards in 14 minutes and 55 seconds.
Water battle and survival test:

In accordance with the test standards of the Navy SEALs, the participants had to complete a fully armed swimming 15 meters, and then abandoned the weapons and equipment back to the shore. And blindfolded to complete the diving at a height of 3 meters, and remove the eye mask to swim back to the shore for the test. If the above tests lose any fixtures, or if they are slightly feared and retreat, they will be eliminated.

Students who pass the preliminary selection will be included in the 4th Ranger Training Camp for training. In addition to continuing to improve physical fitness requirements, there are also the following training subjects:

11 Ranger Stakes courses:

The content is to learn all kinds of light weapons, explosives, performance, operation and maintenance.

20 Darby Queen courses:

The content is to learn from various obstacles beyond.

Marching course:

The content is map use, orientation judgment and day and night march training.

Through all the test participants, they will jump into the facilities known as the Victory Pool to complete the confidence building course, in order to cultivate a high spirit of fighting spirit and mutual support, and the selection of RAP at this stage is also over.

The final stage of training included helicopter rappelling, survival in the wild, leadership development, and raiders assault drills. The Ranger assault drill can be said to be the general acceptance of the basic training. The students will wear the Laser Simulated Combat System (MILES) to experience the war life. Even the captured students will be tortured and asked to learn the survival skills on the battlefield. .

2. Mountain training:

Participants in the basic training will be trained at the 5th Ranger Training Camp in Dahlonega. Participants will receive high-risk mountain training in the Yonah Mountains, the highest peak in Georgia. In addition to continuing to demand physical fitness, students must endure the cold climate of the mountains and continue to train around the clock. The contents are:

Terrain beyond:

First of all, students need to learn a variety of rope knots to use in climbing, assault suspension bridge erection and various drop techniques. The students learn to go beyond all kinds of difficult terrains during the day and night, and if they are not paying attention, they will cause casualties.

Mountain parachute exercise:

Trainees can land safely and accurately in the woods and quickly reach their destination.

Due to the high risk of mountain training, many students are often injured in training, so more than 10% of the students will usually be eliminated.

3. Jungle low-lying training:

Immediately afterwards, the students went to the 6th Ranger Training Camp at Eglin Air Force Base, Florida to receive low-lying training in the jungle. In the primitive jungle full of poisonous snake swamps, the students must survive and fight here. Its content is:

Animal and plant identification training:

Knowing all kinds of animals and plants is a compulsory course for survival in the wild. Participants learn how to avoid snakes and beasts in the jungle and survive in the jungle.

Guerrilla tactical training:

Train the trainees how to penetrate the enemy to complete the mission and the tactical use in the jungle. The students learned about the operation of drowning and small boats in the swamp.

Comprehensive combat exercises:

All the participants were fully armed in the dark, marching from Santa Rosa Island to the Gulf of Mexico and fighting with imaginary enemies. Students who are unable to reach their destination will be eliminated. 4. Summary test:

Finally, according to the Army Physical Fitness Test and the Ranger Barrier Course Standard, students are required to pass 12 physical and technical tests. Participants will pass the black beret and the Ranger armband armband and formally become a member of the Ranger.

Rangers have an average of five days a week, and they are constantly training when there are no tasks. On average, the town war drills are fixed once every six months. At least once a year, large-scale exercises will be held in the mountains, jungles or deserts. And there will be at least two cold and amphibious trainings every three years.

prepared by

Today, the 75th Range Cavalry Corps has about 2,000 soldiers and is affiliated with the US Army Special Operations Command. It has three battalions under its jurisdiction. Its establishment and resident are as follows:

Mission and Mission: Banning Castle, Georgia.
1st Ranger Battalion: Hunter Army Air Base, Georgia.
2nd Ranger Battalion: Luissburg, Washington.
3rd Ranger Battalion: Fort Benning, Georgia.

Each battalion is composed of 580 people, including the battalion department, the battalion company and three infantry companies. One infantry company has 3 infantry platoons with a total of about 152 people and a weapon with about 22 people. One infantry platoon has three infantry classes and one machine gun class. Each class has 1 medical officer. The battalion company includes replenishment, communications, medical services and staff.

Mission Nature Rangers are the strongest light infantry in the United States and can be quickly deployed around the world to cope with the international situation. Every month there will be 1 battalion round for the "Live Cavalry Reserve Force", which must be kept ready at all times. In the event of a situation in the international community, the Rangers Reserve Force will arrive in the area within 18 hours and complete the combat readiness.

Rangeman soldier with M4A1 in active duty metric weaponry

The Rangers are light infantry, so they are not equipped with too many weapons. The common equipment is as follows:

M16A2 rifle
M4A1 rifle

M203 grenade launcher
M249 class machine gun
M82A1 .50 caliber sniper rifle
M9 pistol
84mmRAWS Ranger Anti-armor Weapon
M224 60mm mortar
M-23 mortar trajectory computer
AN/PVS-7b night vision goggles
GPS global satellite locator
BDU jungle camouflage uniform
M65 Jungle Camouflage Jacket
P.A.S.G.T. Kung Fu Dragon Helmet
M12 holster
M40/42 gas mask
LBV tactical vest
AN/PRC-126/127 soldier radio
M19/22 telescope

Under the coordination of the US Special Warfare Command (SOCOM), the Rangers often used the Marine Special Forces, the 82nd Airborne Division, the Delta Force, the Navy Seals, the Air Force Special Forces, and even the non-SOCOM Marine Corps. The investigation team and other units jointly fight. The Rangers, who were self-proclaimed by the special forces, won the trust of the US government. Therefore, in addition to performing special missions, the Rangers often perform general light infantry missions. In the next 21st century, international terrorism and ethnic conflicts continue to erupt. The Rangers, the pioneers of international police, are still ready to travel to foreign countries. Regardless of the truth of the war, the words "Rangers, lead the way!" will always be hidden in the hearts of every Ranger.

REAL AMERICA

www.richardtong.com.au

US NAVY SEALS

Huang Wei, a Chinese engineer at the United States Air and Space Administration's Goddard Space Flight Center, was recently elected a Fellow of the National Academy of Engineering for his invention of the Hilbert-Huang Transform (HHT) method. This is the highest professional honor that American engineers can achieve.

Born in Hubei Province in 1937, he graduated from the Department of Civil Engineering of National Taiwan University in 1960. He received his Ph.D. in fluid mechanics from Johns Hopkins University in 1967. He then served as a marine geologist at the University of Washington. Research Fellow, and Assistant Professor and Associate Professor of the Department of Marine Geography at North Carolina State University, have been working at the Aerospace Department since 1975.

According to a press release issued by the Goddard Space Flight Center in Maryland on March 28th, HHT is a unique spectral analysis method for analyzing non-linear and non-fixed data and images, which can be used for climate cycling, earthquake engineering, and the Earth. Physical detection, submarine design, structural damage detection, satellite data analysis, blood pressure changes, and arrhythmia.

The National Earthquake Engineering Research Center in Taipei is using this method to analyze earthquake risk in various areas of the Taipei Basin. The Aerospace Department also presented the Outstanding Space Action Award to Huang Wei, praising him for "inventing one of the most important applied mathematics methods in the history of the Aeronautics and Astronautics Department."

Huang has published about 90 reviewed papers and has been the assistant editor of the Journal of Natural Marine Geography since 1990.

www.richardtong.com.au

CHINESE IN AMERICA

LI WENHE LIVING IN A PARADISE

"They desperately want others to believe that my father made a terrible mistake." Li Wenhe's daughter Li Chunyi said that she was almost crying. She paused a little and then raised her voice: "But he is not wrong! He is just doing his job. He is innocent."

Nearly 200 listeners who participated in the fundraising activities of Li Wen and the defense fund in Silicon Valley immediately gave warm applause, and many people took out the check.

The Los Angeles Times reported that Silicon Valley Asians recently supported Li Wenhe's situation. Li Wenhe's children and relatives and friends in the support of Li Wen and the fundraising meeting told Li Wenhe that people did not know.

Software engineer, 26-year-old Li Chunyi said that his father was overwhelmed by the allegations. "He lives completely in his own world, never reads newspapers or watches TV. He always trusts others and is willing to help others. He is too naive."

In addition to the work in the laboratory, Li Wenhe cooks, cleans and other household chores for the whole family. He also grows vegetables in the backyard and goes fishing on weekends. In addition, he likes to enjoy Mozart's music, Hugo, Flaubert and Dickens.

The US federal judge recently decided that the nuclear physicist Li Wenhe, who was employed by the US government, was tried on November 6. Li Wenhe was accused of illegally copying US nuclear weapons secrets.

Li Wenhe, 60, was arrested in December last year for allegedly downloading and copying nuclear weapons from the computer at Los Alamos National Laboratory. He was dismissed from the Alabama National Laboratory last March. Li Wenhe claimed that he had destroyed the tapes of unknown origin, but the judiciary pointed out that Li's argument was not supported by evidence. Li Wenhe's appeal was heard in the Denver Court of Appeal, but it was decided that he could not be released on bail before he was tried because it was alleged that several of his computer tapes had not been found.

The Los Angeles Times reported that Li Wenhe was born in 1939 in a poor farm in Nantou, Taiwan, with ten brothers and sisters. During the Second World War, the Japanese soldiers had severely interrogated Li Wenhe about the whereabouts of his parents. He said that he will never forget the fear at the time.

Shortly after the Second World War, Li Wenhe's elderly parents passed away. Li Wen and his relatives went to study in northern Taiwan and later entered the successful university. In September 1964, he entered Texas A&M University.

Although he has lived in the United States for more than 30 years, Li Wenhe is still an introverted shy person, and he is not fluent in English. But he adapted to the United States quite quickly. He participated in the football team at the university, opened the blue Mustang, received a master's degree in 1966, received his Ph.D. in 1969, and joined the Los Alamos National Laboratory in 1980. And was assigned to the top secret department in the design of nuclear warheads.

The secret world of Los Alamos soon became the core of Li Wen and his family. His wife took the most confidential work in the lab until she was a computer programmer there before she retired in 1995. His son received a lower-level contact secret permit to test the computer code during the summer vacation at the University of California, San Diego. His daughter specializes in English during the University of California at Los Angeles, and also handles data for the Nevada Nuclear Test Base during the summer vacation.

Li Wen and his family lived in a secluded street in Baishi Town.

But by 1996, Li Wenhe's peaceful life was suddenly shrouded in a shadow--the Department of Energy officials believed that Los Alamos leaked the US's highest nuclear warheads to China. Li Wenhe, who was approved by the laboratory and visited China twice in 1986 and 1988, was the focus of the FBI investigation.

According to the report, the FBI, in addition to using a variety of improper means to deal with Li Wenhe, also launched a sudden attack on Li Wenhe's relatives. Li Chunyi said, is simply the way they used "" The Godfather "direct replica." Last June 9, the FBI were living in several cities of Wen Ho Lee's daughter, son, brother, brother, niece, etc. At the same time, the family searched and asked them to go to the grand jury to testify on June 18.

In order to determine Li Wenhe's motives for leaking, the FBI repeatedly questioned Li Wenhe's financial and living habits, including lending his brother $16,000.

Li Wenhe's son, Li Zhong, said, "They know that we often drive to California and stay in Las Vegas. In fact, the reason is that mom likes buffets and shopping. So Dad and I go to the casino to kill time. They want to know if my dad lost a lot of money, so I lacked money. They asked me how much he lost at most. I told them that I had seen him very sad after losing a fifty dollar, and then it was very long. Time is not playing in the casino."

The descriptions of Li Chunyi and Li Zhong not only won sympathy and applause, but many people have been on the spot. At a meeting of less than 200 people, people donated 23,000 yuan. Since Li Wenhe's arrest on December 10 last year, Li Wenhe's defense fund has received nearly 290,000 yuan in donations.

www.richardtong.com.au

ILLEGAL CHINESE IMMIGRANTS LIVING IN THE SHADOW OF THE UNDERWORLD

Thousands of Chinese illegal immigrants are cruelly exploited in Chinese restaurants in the United States and garment factories known as "sweatshops." It is estimated that about 100,000 Chinese illegal immigrants are doing the worst jobs in big cities in the United States. In New York, about 35,000 people work 18 hours a day, sometimes only $1 an hour, which is only 1/6 of the US minimum wage. They seem to be invisible, mixed among the 500,000 Asians in New York.

These illegal immigrants were brought to the United States by the gang of trafficked people and were outside the American society. They concentrated on "Chinatown" in New York, Chicago, San Francisco and Los Angeles. For many illegal immigrants, the life of Chinatown is not as attractive as the film depicts. In addition to the hard work every day, they live in dilapidated houses, and several people take turns using a bed. While some people work, others sleep. The cruel exploitation of these Chinese people plays a role in regulating the price of the New York market. Chinese restaurants have the lowest prices because the wages for chefs and waiters are extremely low. The clothes produced by the "sweatshop" are also very cheap.

Many consumers are satisfied, but they don't understand the real life of illegal Chinese immigrants. The smuggling of immigrants is controlled by many underworld organizations. Now these organizations have headquarters with charity brands, and everything on the surface is legal. There are dozens of underworld organizations engaged in illegal immigration activities, each of which is associated with a group in mainland China or Taiwan. After the triads carried illegal immigrants into the United States through smuggling activities only known to them, they arranged to work in restaurants or garment factories and began to exploit them.

In Chinatown, not far from Wall Street, it is easy to encounter such illegal immigrants who are enslaved and intimidated. They all follow the principle of silence and rarely talk to Westerners. A female hawker described her tragic experience: "I paid $38,000 for coming to the United States." She is not old, her hair is not combed, her nails are covered with nail polish, she wears cheap shirts and worn shoes. , sitting on the fence of the building and selling phone cards.

How much money she got from her like this. She explained: "Before I came, I sold myself to the underworld." The underworld smuggled her into the United States, but she had the right to exploit her until she could pay off her debts or get rid of the underworld control. She first worked in a "sweatshop". "I give my salary to them every week, only to have some food," she said with no expression. "I work from 7 am every day until 1 am the next day. Every month must be handed over to them. $1,000. "After three years, when she thought she had paid off her debts, the triads began to ask her for interest, and they had to pay them $1,000 a month.

Later she got rid of the control of the underworld. She said: "Now I work for myself but I must be wary of them and the Immigration Bureau, because if I get caught, or killed, or sent back to China, I don't know which is worse."

Since August 1997, at lunch and dinner, more than 20 people have marched in Chinatown, demanding to improve the working conditions of Chinese immigrants and to get the right to work 8 hours a day and get a minimum wage. But no one cares about them. It's easy to understand that except for the small scope of illegal immigration, the whole problem involves the salary and tip of the 35,000 people, and their income is lower than the ticket for the Yankees baseball team. The 35-year-old Li Ling was born in Fujian and has been in the United States for five years. He said: "We want to show the Americans that here, just under their noses, there are the last slaves of the 20th century." There is a chef in the parade. For four years, he went from 9:00 to the first every day. At 1 am on the second day, there is no right to rest, and the hourly wage is $1. He said: "At that time, when I went to sleep, I was exhausted and had no time to think about the problem. I think the United States is like this."

A 40-year-old woman working at the "sweatshop" spoke about her adventures. She took a boat from China to Hong Kong six years ago. There, it was in contact with a drug trafficking group. Take a fishing boat to the United States. "My sister died on the boat and was thrown into the sea. On the night of arriving in the United States, the boat turned over. I swam 200 meters before landing. I was separated from my husband on the beach and I never saw him again." While talking, doing work. She complained: "The hope is so great, it has suffered so much, and the result is still the same."

www.richardtong.com.au

MANAGEMENT GENIUS ZHANG SHENGKAI

Zhang Shengkai, the current president of the World Federation of Taiwan Chambers of Commerce, is an entrepreneur who is known throughout the world as a "business genius" by Wall Street. He is also an enthusiastic development of global Taiwanese organizations, starting with compassion and serving the community. Leader.

Zhang Shengkai graduated from the Department of Chemistry of Taiwan University and obtained a master's degree in food chemistry from Imperial University of Tokyo, Japan. He studied in Japan in 1972 and then immigrated to Brazil and began to engage in the import trade of molasses. After three years, due to the stable sales volume, it has invested in the factory. At first, it only supplied other factories as raw materials. Because of its high quality and low price, it was put into the market for seven years. After the biggest competitor, the American company Albert Pharmaceuticals, lost its competitiveness, it stopped the raw materials factory and changed to Zhang Shengkai's Fangda. Company procurement. At this time, Fangda has sold more than 80% of the world's sugar molasses, ranking first in the world.

In 1983, Fangda began to work with its largest customer, Swiss YEPE, to enter the low-calorie sugar market. Zhang Shengkai broke through the blind spot of low-calorie sugar sales, and launched it as a food image, breaking the stereotypes of such products sold only in pharmacies, changing to large-capacity, new-looking packaging, displaying in supermarkets, repositioning products, selling Pipes have also soared. Since then, "Fangda" low-calorie sugar foods have been the market leader, with an annual turnover of more than 50 million US dollars.

In 1997, the Wall Street Journal reported that the paper diapers produced by the Chinese-born Zhang Shengkai's YENKO company had emerged in Brazil, and the image of cheap and good quality successfully defeated the world's two giants: Johnson & Johnson. (Jiaosheng) and Procter & Gamble (Boao), boarded the Brazilian diaper sales champion. In the consumer market of Brazil with 160 million people, Kimberly Clark, which produces high-quality sanitary products, decided to purchase 5 percent of YENKO, which was founded by Zhang Shengkai only six years after careful investigation. Ten shares, injecting research and development technology into it, and using its existing marketing channels to create a win-win situation, prompted the company's annual turnover to reach $330 million.

Twelve years ago, Zhang Shengkai founded the "Sao Paulo Overseas Chinese Association" to contact the township. In the cold winters of South America in June and July each year, other overseas Chinese associations are invited to hold the overseas Chinese winter relief charity activities to directly help the cold and return to Brazilian society. Although he has not been appointed as president in recent years, he has been greatly assisted. This activity has already become a major event in the local overseas Chinese community, indirectly enhancing the good image of the Chinese and promoting good national diplomacy.

Ten years ago, Zhang Shengkai suffered from thyroid cancer and returned to health after surgery. He discovered that the self-learning of Satan in Buddhism is the spiritual destination that he pursued throughout his life. In 1992, when the Xingyun Master first brought his son to Brazil to promote the Fa, Zhang Shengkai would donate his nearly four thousand ping private villas, and asked the Master Nebula to send a Master to establish a "Rulai Temple" and with the Buddhist friends. Together with the purchase of the 10,000-pound land opposite the Rulai Temple, the "Brazil Foguang Association" was established.

For more than six years, the Brazilian Foguang Association has owned the "Foguang Chinese Literature Garden" with the active planning and membership of Zhang Shengkai and others. There are basketball courts, football fields, four tennis courts and two swimming pools. Every Sunday has become The important venues for overseas Chinese study, entertainment and networking are the two groups of the Brazilian Overseas Chinese Tennis and Basketball Association, which often hold various competitions.

The World Taiwan Chamber of Commerce was jointly established in 1994, with North America, Asia, Europe, Africa, Central and South America, and Oceania as the organizational unit of the existing Taiwan Chamber of Commerce. Under each unit, there are nearly 100 local city chambers of commerce in more than 40 countries, with more than 20,000 members. In September 1998, Zhang Shengkai was elected as the president of the World Chamber of Commerce in Taiwan.

Since taking office, Zhang Shengkai's servants have traveled to various parts of the world to communicate with Taiwanese businessmen, and established an online communication system for overseas Taiwanese business information. He also promoted the Taiwanese business--the second generation of young Taiwanese businessmen to build a joint system, which was held with Jiage. Youth Taiwan Business Entrepreneurship Seminar; In February this year, a grand meeting of the World Federation of Taiwanese Businessmen in Brazil was held to bring the global Taiwanese business organization to a further development.

www.richardtong.com.au

AIDS BUSTER HE DAY I

He Dayi, born with a child's face, is actually 48 years old this year.

The man of the year 1996

In 1970, when he was studying at the California Institute of Technology, he often stayed at the Las Vegas Casino, where he used his amazing memory to promote the casino and even was expelled several times. Today, He Dayi is still like a gambler, but his opponent is AIDS. He is the director of the Aaron AIDS Research Center in New York City. In 1996, he published the latest strategy at the 11th International AIDS Symposium and was selected by Time magazine as "The Man of the Year 1996".

Negating the "latency period" theory The medical profession used to think that when the HIV virus enters the human body, it will lurk for three to ten years, and then I do not know what was driven, and suddenly launched a death attack. In 1994, He Dayi showed that this view was wrong, and the incubation period did not exist. In the sudden period of time, it was the human immune system that was stubbornly resistant to the virus.

In 1979, He Dayi received his doctorate in medicine at Harvard Medical School. Two years later, AIDS became popular. He was a resident doctor at the Sinai Medical College in Luo Province and has seen many homosexual patients. He Dayi first suspected that AIDS is caused by a virus. In 1982, he moved to the Massachusetts Institute of Virology, Boston, to follow the "Ma Tian Boots" for research. Because of the funding, he has to go to the hospital clinic as a night doctor. During this period, he saw many patients who had a cold, could not detect a cold virus in the blood, but found the HIV virus.

So, He Dayi found four gay patients who were suffering from a cold and tested blood for him. Initially, a large number of HIV were found; but after a few weeks, it suddenly dropped to an unmeasurable level. He suspects that the virus is hidden in the lymph nodes and may be replicating. He initially thought that the rate of replication was millions of times a day, and the patient's immune system continually wiped them out; but one day, the immune system was exhausted, and suddenly it was like a dyke, and it was out of control.

In order to prove this situation, He Dayi developed a strategy. In 1994, he applied a formula called Protease to patients; he believed that if his theory was correct, the virus would stop breeding, and the antibodies produced by the human immune system would suddenly increase due to inertia. As expected, it is shocking that the virus replicates in the incubation period at a rate of hundreds of millions per day. No wonder the immune cells in the body, the casualties are heavy.

It must be pre-emptive. The former medical community believed that AIDS was attacked when it just woke up from a dormant state. He Dayi proved that it was too late. To overcome the virus, it must be preemptive in the early days. In 1995, He Dayi published this amazing discovery in the "Nature Magazine".

Re-injection against the virus

In recent years, there is a drug called AZT that deals with HIV, but it is more tenacious if there is a fish that slips through the net. He Dayi decided to make a next big bet, combining AZT, Protease inhibitors and a drug called 3TC, and the chance of success is estimated to be 10 million. As a result, the new drug worked. Of the ten patients, seven have disappeared, other complications have improved, and damaged tissue can also be repaired by transplantation.

Continue to pursue victory

Although He Dayi has been successful, he believes that the virus may be lurking in brain tissue and spinal fluid, so patients must use it for life. The only concern is that the virus invades the cell's chromosomes, so the stronger drugs are useless. Now, He Dayi continues his research and hopes to pursue the victory and annihilate AIDS.

Contact Us lechuantong@gmail.com

REAL AMERICA

Richard Tong

www.richardtong.com.au

Printed in the USA
CPSIA information can be obtained
at www.ICGtesting.com
CBHW042355071224
18641CB00049B/657